The Zen of Ziggy ®

Other Ziggy Books

Ziggy & Friends
Ziggy Faces Life
Ziggy's Big Little Book
Life Is Just a Bunch of Ziggys
Alphabet Soup Isn't Supposed to Make Sense
Ziggy's Place
Ziggy's Ups and Downs
Ziggy in the Fast Lane
Ziggy's Follies
Ziggy's School of Hard Knocks
Ziggy on the Outside Looking In...
Look Out World...Here I Come!
Ziggy...A Rumor in His Own Time
A Day in the Life of Ziggy...
1-800-ZIGGY
My Life as a Cartoon
The Z Files
Ziggy's Divine Comedy
Get Ziggy with It
Ziggy's Friends for Life

The Ziggy Treasury
Encore! Encore!!
Ziggy's Star Performances
The First 25 Years Are the Hardest

The Zen of Ziggy®

A ZIGGY® COLLECTION

by Tom Wilson

**Andrews McMeel
Publishing**

Kansas City

For information, write Andrews McMeel Publishing, an Andrews McMeel Universal company, 4520 Main Street, Kansas City, Missouri 64111.

www.uComics.com and www.andrewsmcmeel.com

02 03 04 05 06 BAH 10 9 8 7 6 5 4 3 2 1

ISBN: 0-7407-2324-3

Library of Congress Catalog Control Number: 2001095912

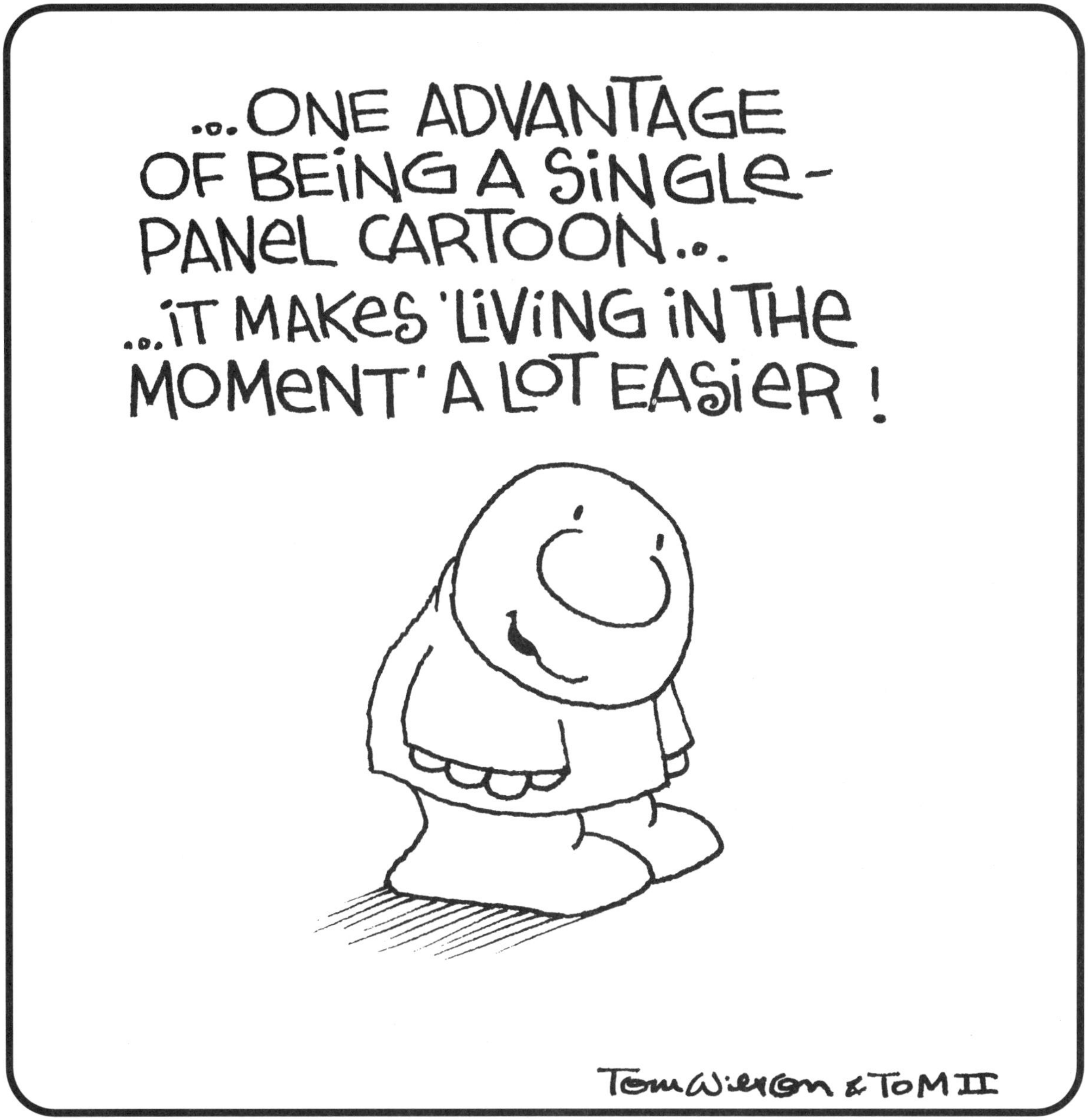
...ONE ADVANTAGE OF BEING A SINGLE-PANEL CARTOON...
...IT MAKES 'LIVING IN THE MOMENT' A LOT EASIER!
TOM WILSON & TOM II

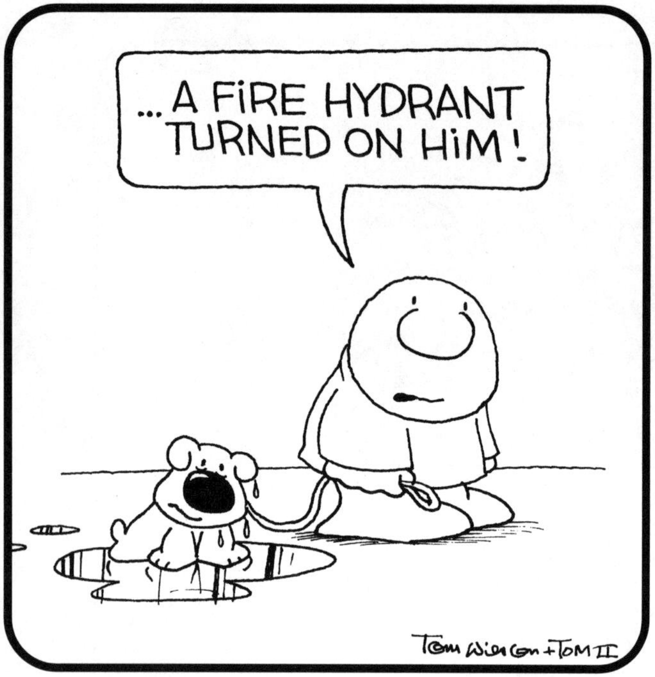
...A FIRE HYDRANT TURNED ON HIM!
Tom Wilson + Tom II

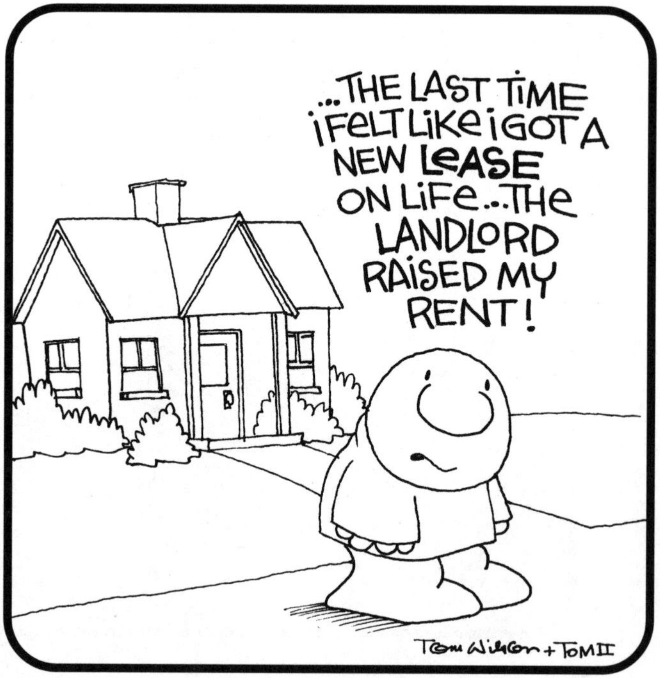
...THE LAST TIME I FELT LIKE I GOT A NEW LEASE ON LIFE...THE LANDLORD RAISED MY RENT!
Tom Wilson + Tom II

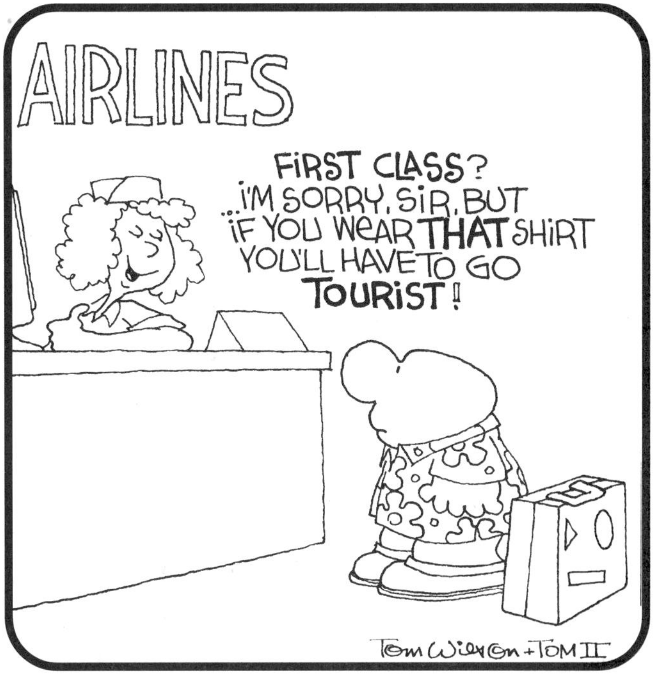
AIRLINES
FIRST CLASS? ...I'M SORRY, SIR, BUT IF YOU WEAR THAT SHIRT YOU'LL HAVE TO GO TOURIST!
Tom Wilson + TOM II

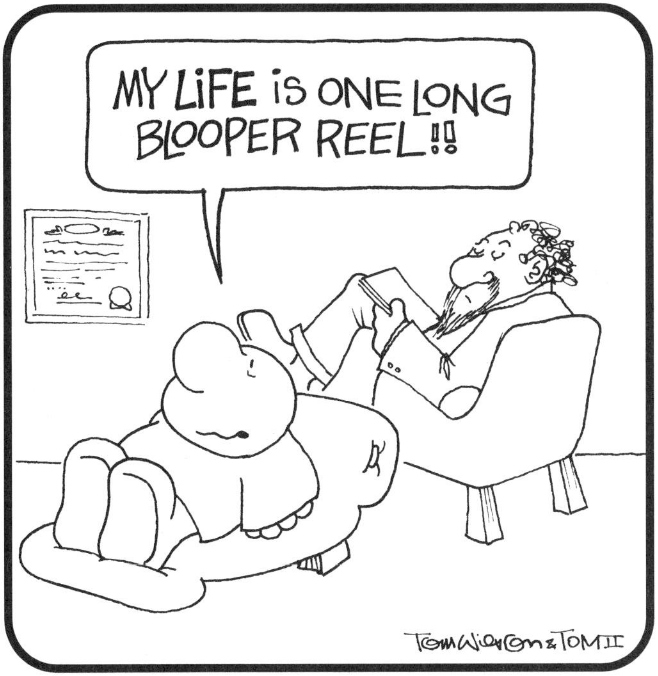
MY LIFE IS ONE LONG BLOOPER REEL!!
Tom Wilson & TOM II

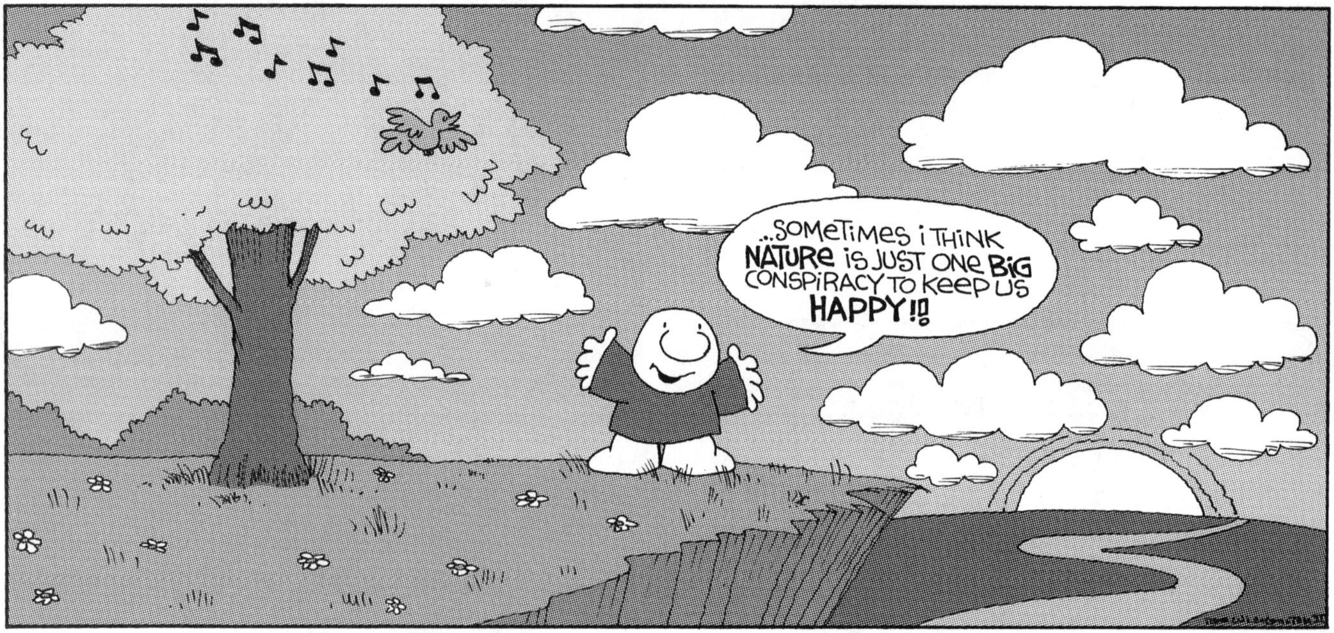
...SOMETIMES I THINK NATURE IS JUST ONE BIG CONSPIRACY TO KEEP US HAPPY!!

TO:

HAPPY VALENTINE'S DAY!

FROM:

PMG, Inc.
FKFK19H051

valentines@papermagic.com

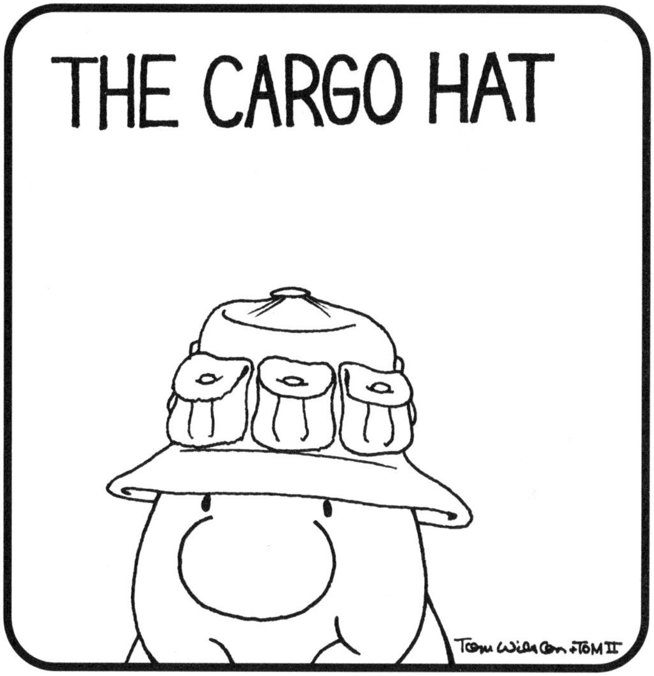
THE CARGO HAT
Tom Wilson + TOM II

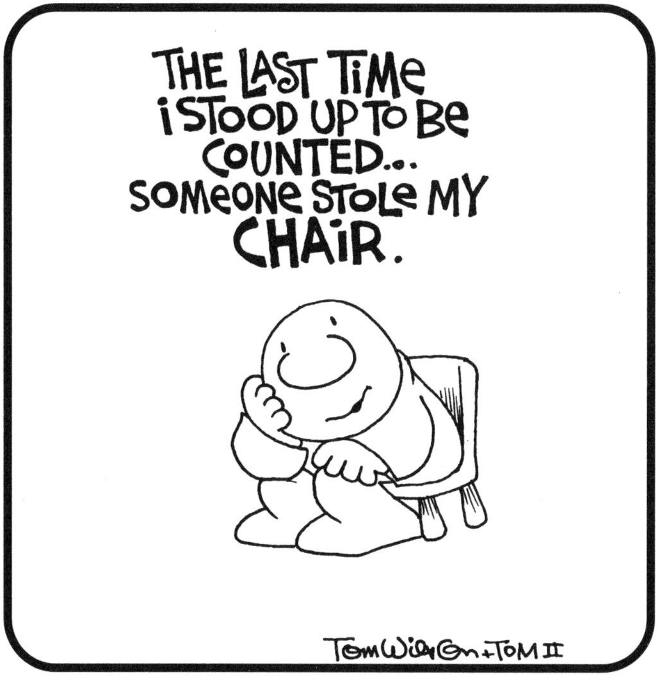
THE LAST TIME I STOOD UP TO BE COUNTED... SOMEONE STOLE MY CHAIR.
Tom Wilson + TOM II

...IT'S NO SURPRISE THE 'GOOD OLD DAYS' SEEM BETTER THAN THE PRESENT. ...THEY'VE SPENT MORE TIME IN EDITING!!

Tom Wilson + Tom II

...THEY SAY: "DO WHAT YOU *LOVE* AND THE **MONEY** WILL **FOLLOW**"... ...BUT MINE FOLLOWS SO FAR BEHIND, IT NEVER CATCHES UP WITH ME!!

Tom Wilson + Tom II

Y'KNOW, JOSH, LOOKING UP AT THE NIGHT SKY ALWAYS MAKES ME FEEL SO SMALL!
JUST THINK, WE'RE ALL TINY SPECKS ON THIS PLANET!
...AND THIS PLANET IS JUST A SMALL DOT IN OUR SOLAR SYSTEM!
...AND OUR SUN IS JUST A POINT OF LIGHT IN OUR GALAXY...
...A GALAXY, WHICH ITSELF IS JUST ANOTHER SPECK AMONG BILLIONS OF GALAXIES IN THE UNIVERSE!
...IT'S AMAZING HOW SMALL EACH OF US REALLY IS!
WHAT I FIND AMAZING IS HOW YOU GO THROUGH THIS WHOLE ROUTINE EVERY TIME YOU GAIN A FEW POUNDS.

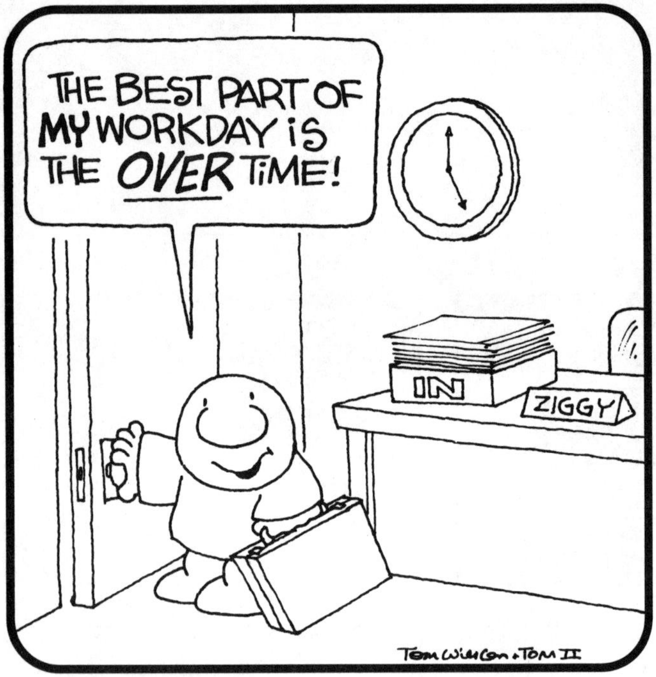
THE BEST PART OF MY WORKDAY IS THE OVER TIME!
IN
ZIGGY
TOM WILSON & TOM II

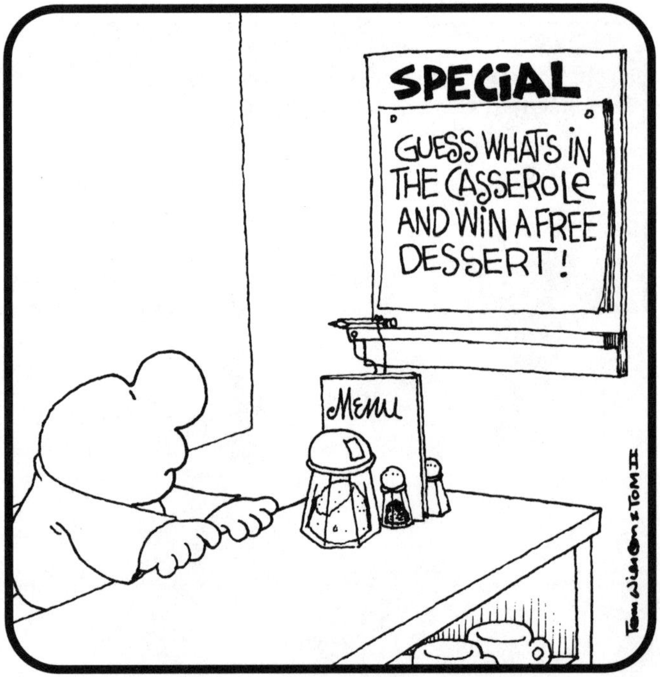
SPECIAL
GUESS WHAT'S IN THE CASSEROLE AND WIN A FREE DESSERT!
MENU
TOM WILSON & TOM II

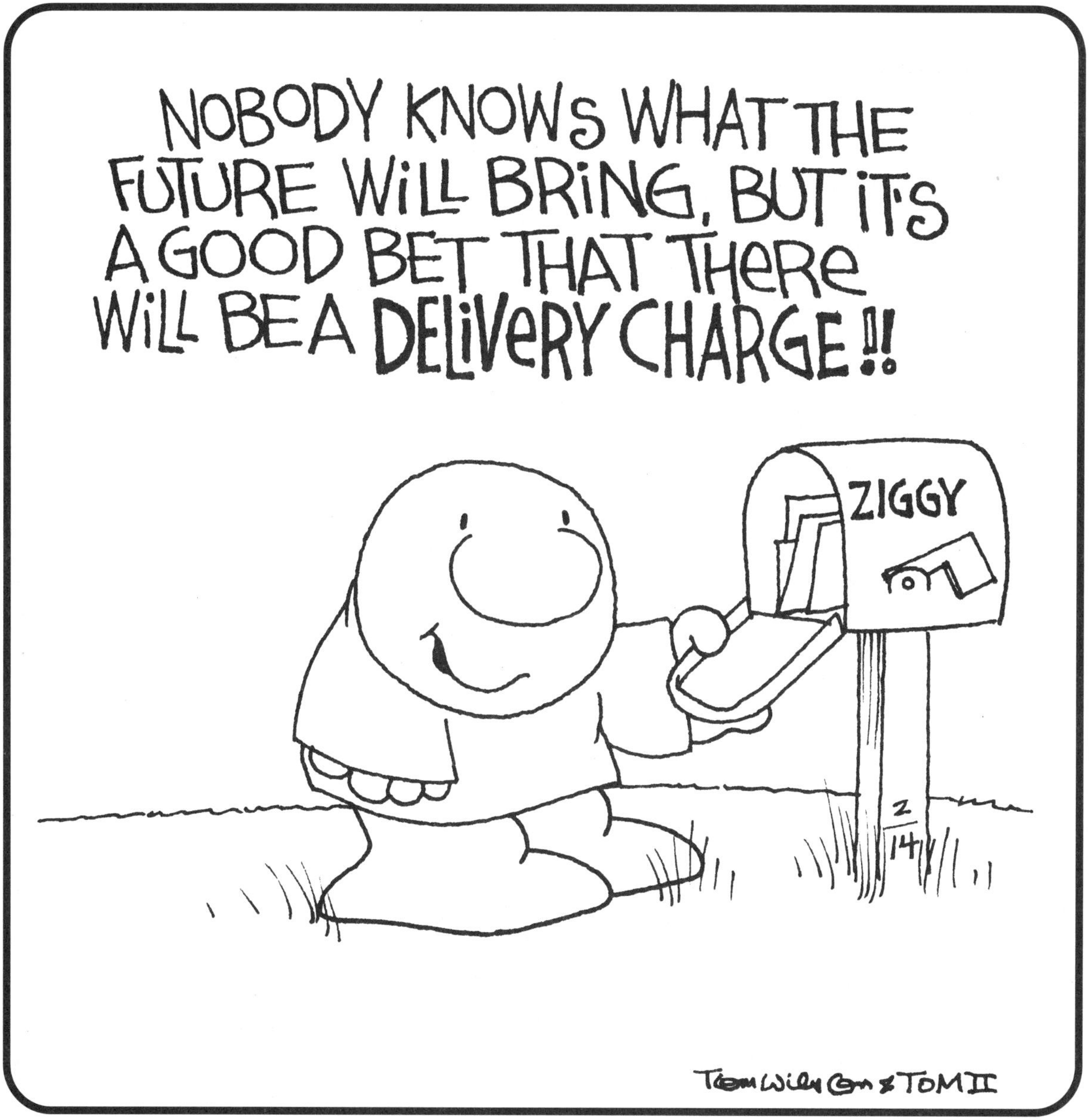
NOBODY KNOWS WHAT THE FUTURE WILL BRING, BUT IT'S A GOOD BET THAT THERE WILL BE A DELIVERY CHARGE!!
ZIGGY
2/14
Tom Wilson & TOM II

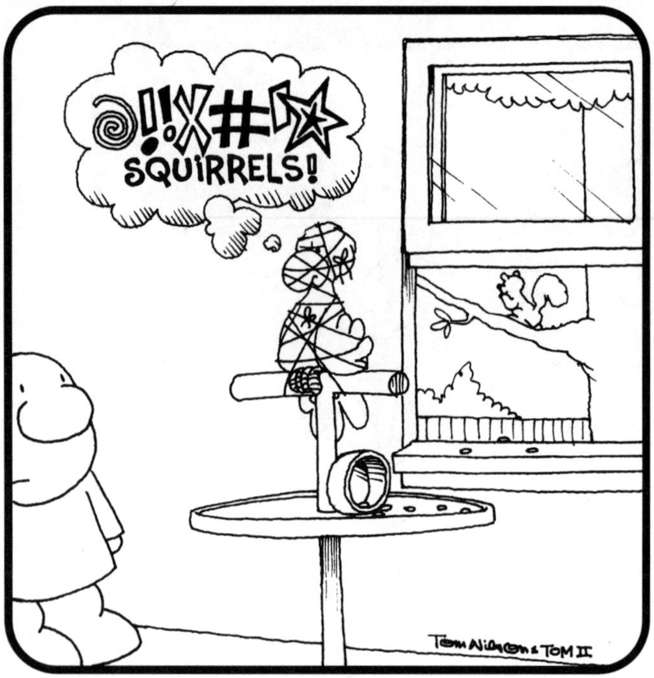
@!X#☆
SQUIRRELS!
Tom Wilson & TOM II

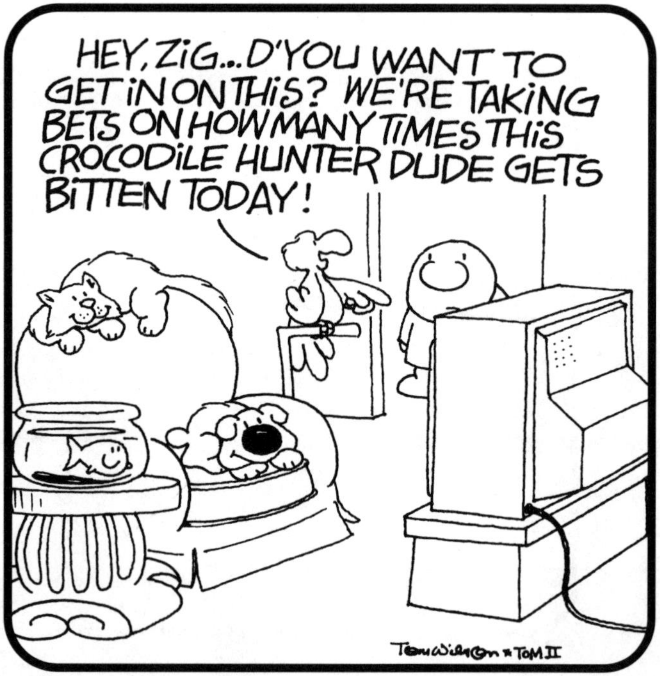
HEY, ZIG... D'YOU WANT TO GET IN ON THIS? WE'RE TAKING BETS ON HOW MANY TIMES THIS CROCODILE HUNTER DUDE GETS BITTEN TODAY!
Tom Wilson & TOM II

ZIGGY, SINCE YOUR FEAR OF FLYING IS SUBCONSCIOUS, I MUST ENTER YOUR SUBCONSCIOUS!
...YOU'RE...GETTING...SLEEEEPY...
ZIGGY..WHEN YOU WAKE, YOU WON'T JUST KNOW THAT FLYING IS AS SAFE AS WALKING YOU'LL BELIEVE IT'S AS SAFE!!...JUST AS SAFE AS WALKING...
...THANKS, DOCTOR... I FEEL LIKE A NEW MAN!
KNOCK
KNOCK
KNOCK
NOW, I'M AFRAID OF WALKING!!
TOM WILSON + TOM II

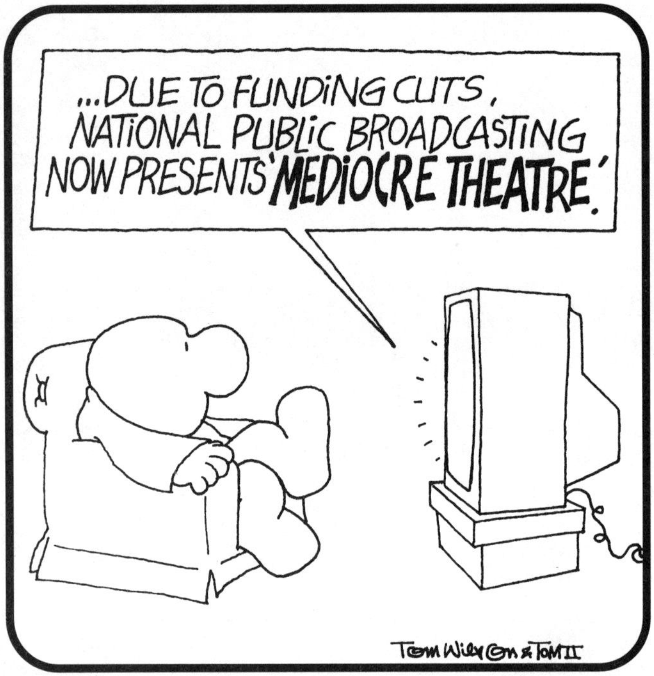
...DUE TO FUNDING CUTS, NATIONAL PUBLIC BROADCASTING NOW PRESENTS 'MEDIOCRE THEATRE.'
Tom Wilson & Tom II

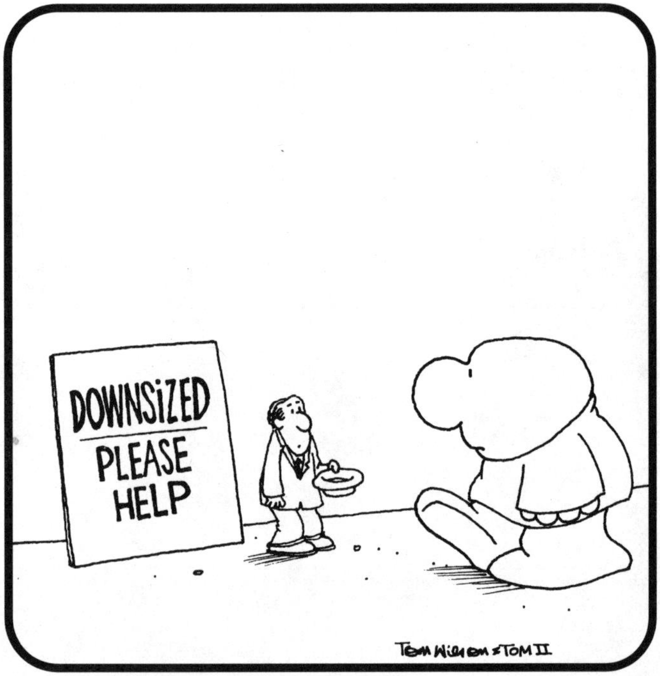
DOWNSIZED
PLEASE HELP
Tom Wilson & Tom II

OOPS!
..UH-OH..
..I'M STUCK!
..SOMEBODY HELP THIS POOR MAN!
RESCUE
NEWS 7
..I SHOULD'VE FIGURED THAT MY 15 MINUTES OF FAME WOULD COME AT A BAD TIME!!

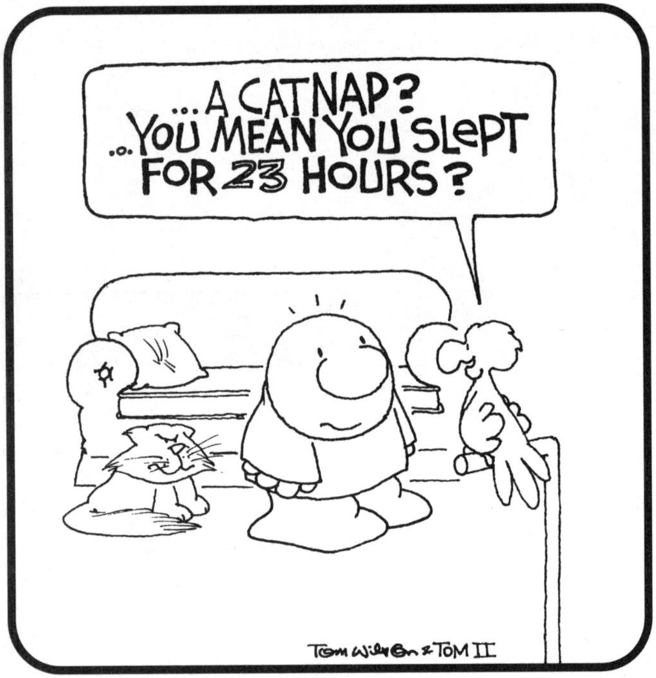
...A CATNAP?
...YOU MEAN YOU SLEPT FOR 23 HOURS?
Tom Wilson & TOM II

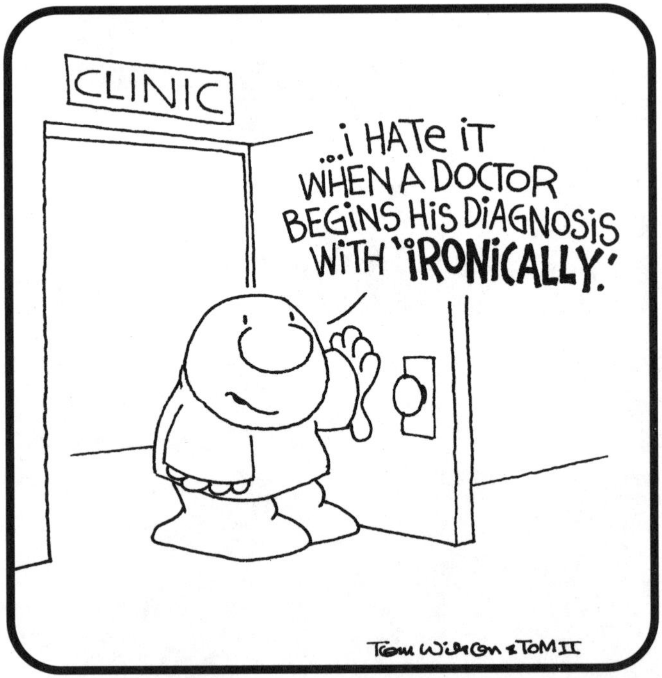
CLINIC
...I HATE IT WHEN A DOCTOR BEGINS HIS DIAGNOSIS WITH 'IRONICALLY.'
Tom Wilson & TOM II

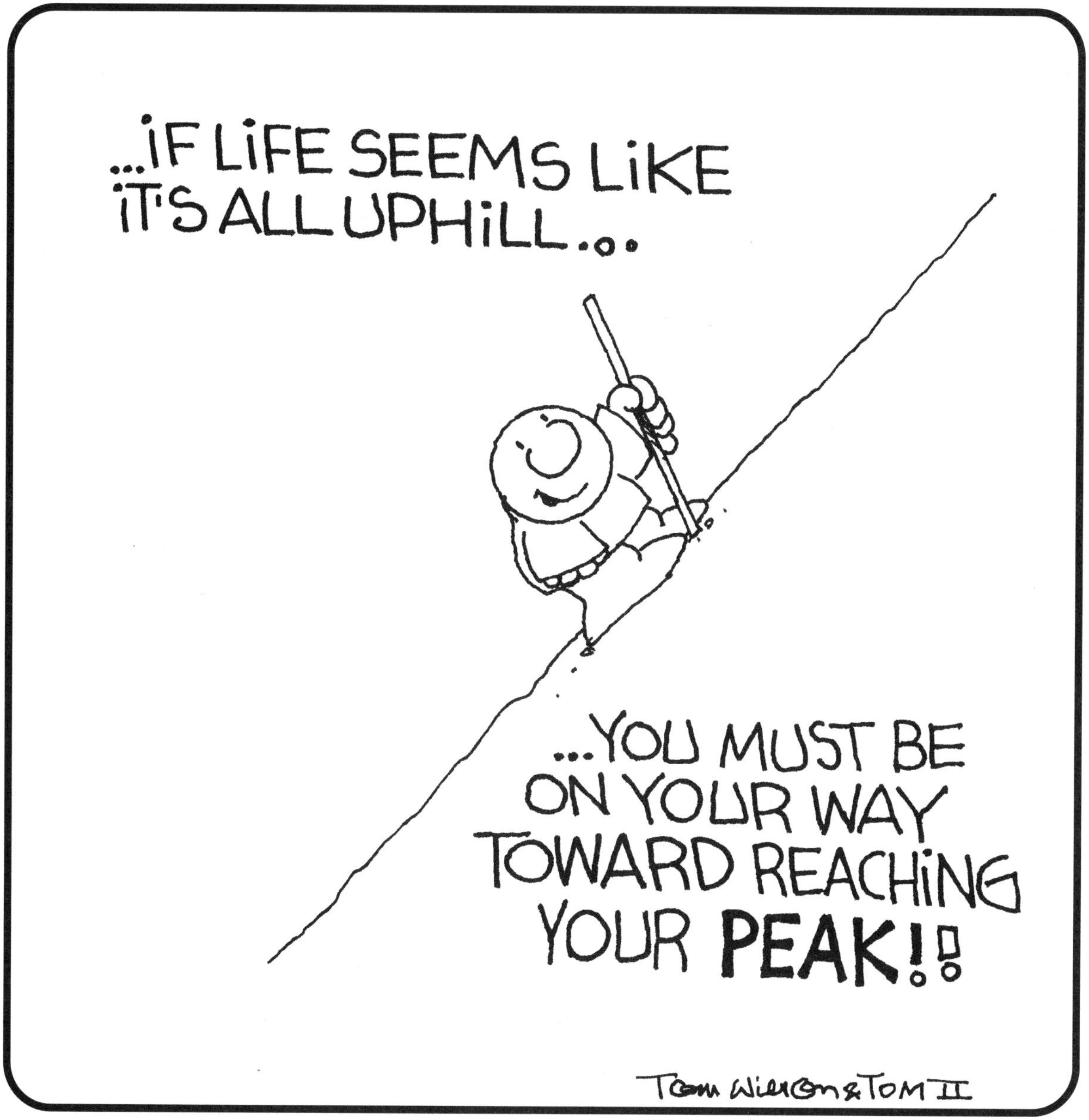
...IF LIFE SEEMS LIKE IT'S ALL UPHILL...
...YOU MUST BE ON YOUR WAY TOWARD REACHING YOUR PEAK!!
Tom Wilson & Tom II

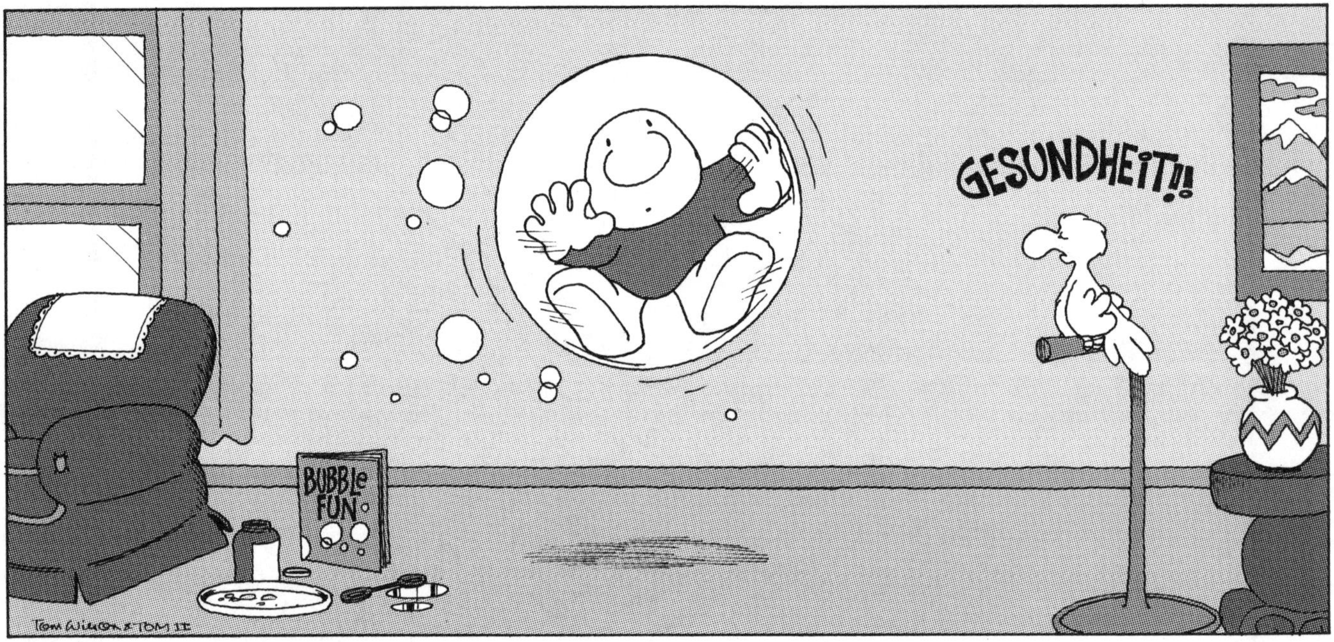
GESUNDHEIT!!
BUBBLE FUN
TOM WILSON & TOM II

..HEY, FUZZ-
CAN YOU BRING
ME THE PAPER?
ULP!
PUFF
PUFF
FRONT PAGE
LOCAL NEWS
..PANT..
..PANT..
..PANT..
LOCAL NEWS
CLASSIFIEDS
FLOP!
CLASSIFIEDS
i LOVE SUNDAYS!
..i HATE SUNDAYS!
SPORTS
COMICS

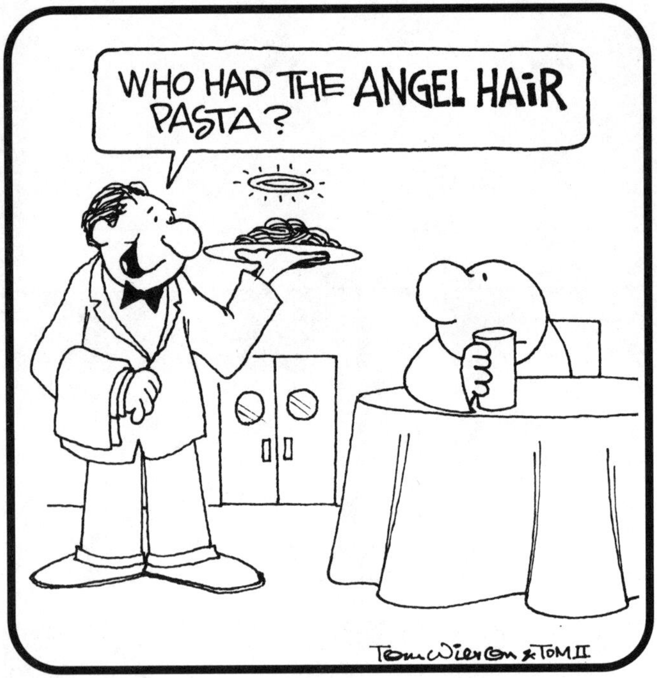
WHO HAD THE ANGEL HAIR PASTA?
Tom Wilson & TOM II

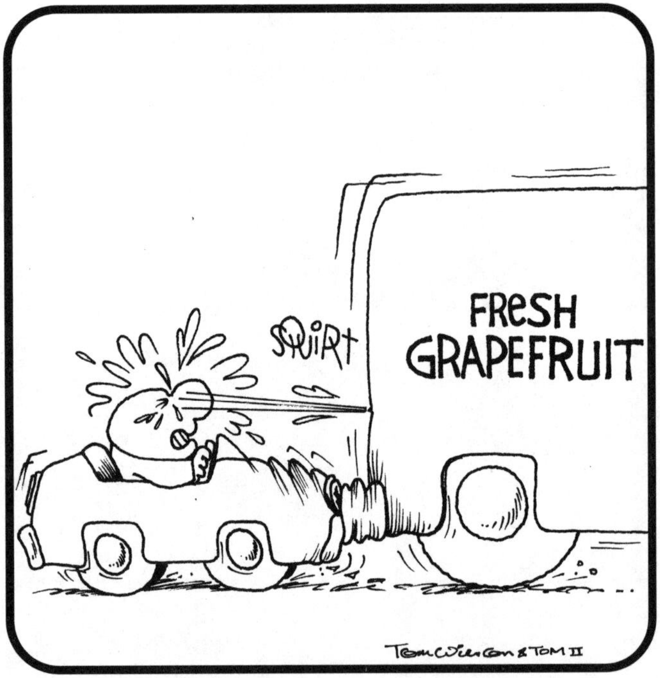
SQUIRT
FRESH GRAPEFRUIT
Tom Wilson & TOM II

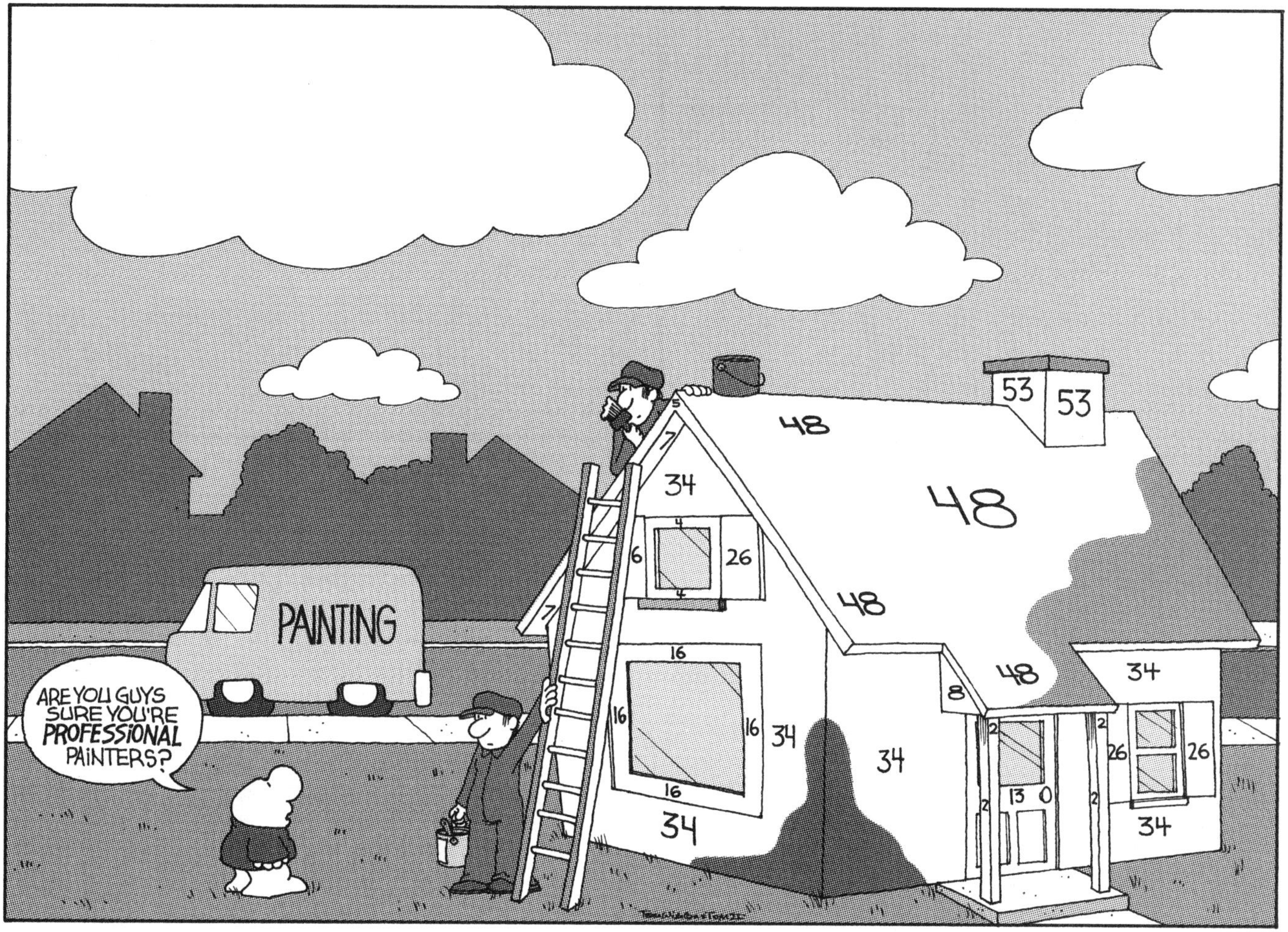
ARE YOU GUYS SURE YOU'RE **PROFESSIONAL** PAINTERS?
PAINTING

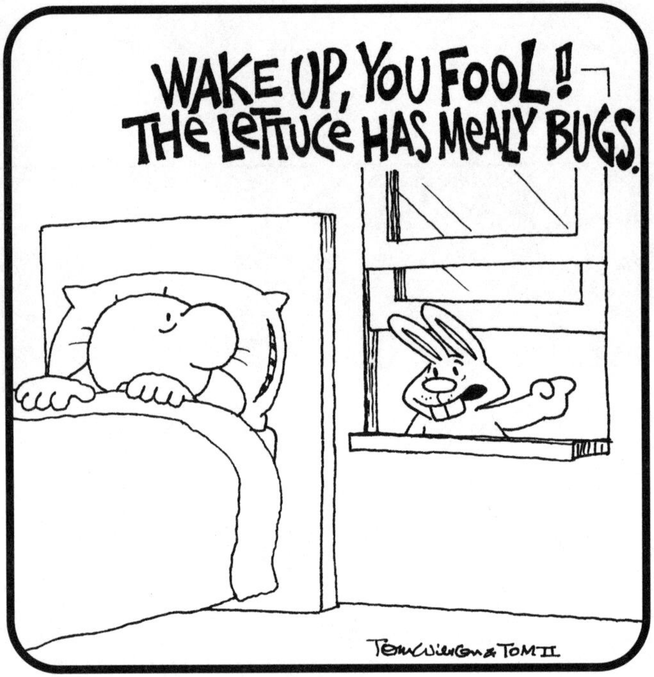
WAKE UP, YOU FOOL! THE LETTUCE HAS MEALY BUGS.
TOM WILSON & TOM II

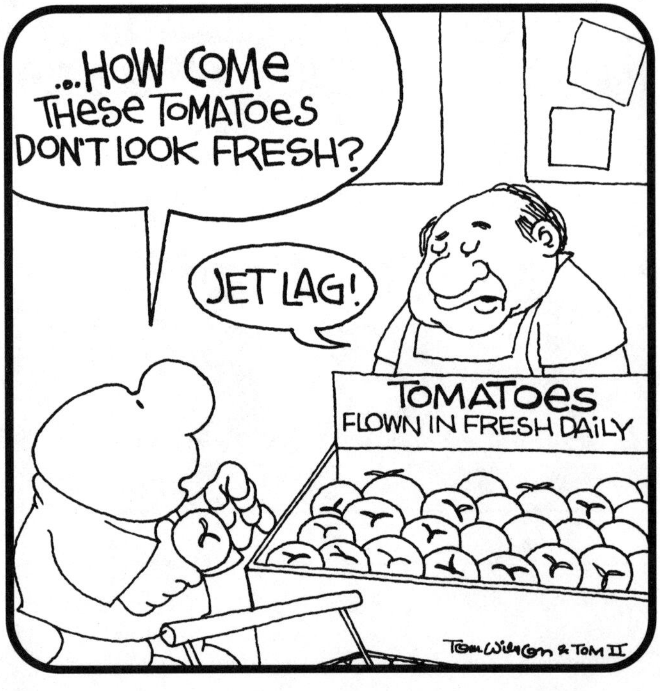
...HOW COME THESE TOMATOES DON'T LOOK FRESH?
JET LAG!
TOMATOES
FLOWN IN FRESH DAILY
TOM WILSON & TOM II

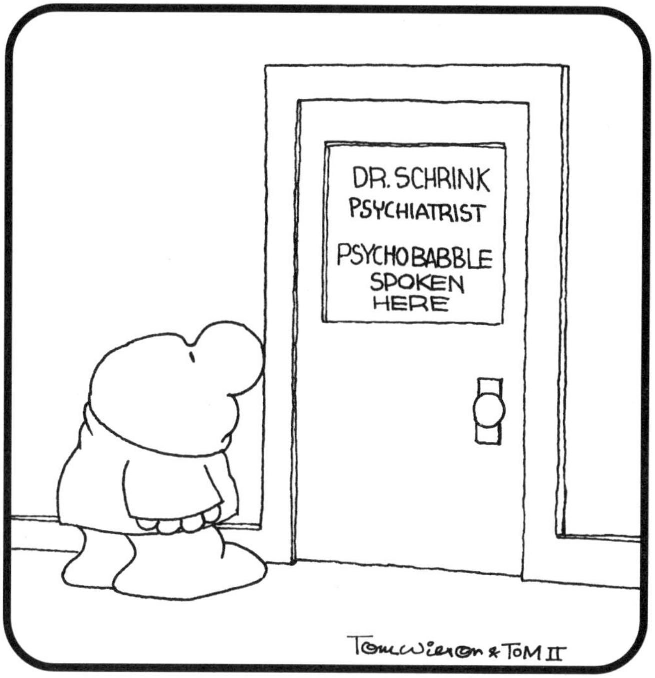
DR. SCHRINK
PSYCHIATRIST
PSYCHOBABBLE
SPOKEN
HERE
Tom Wilson & TOM II

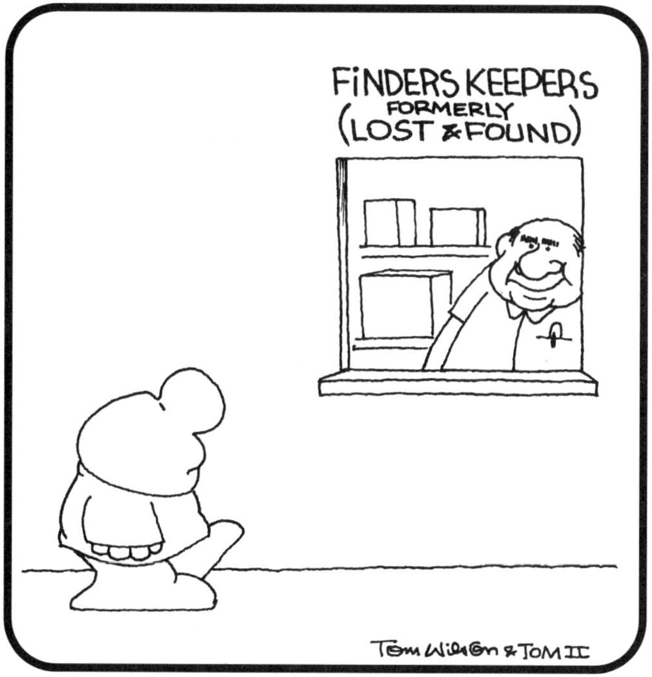
FINDERS KEEPERS
FORMERLY
(LOST & FOUND)
Tom Wilson & TOM II

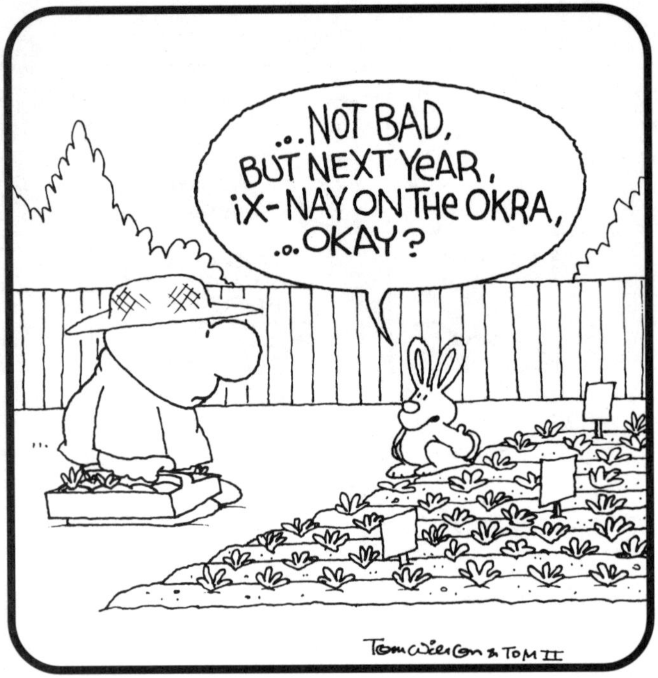
...NOT BAD,
BUT NEXT YEAR,
IX-NAY ON THE OKRA,
...OKAY?
TOM WILSON & TOM II

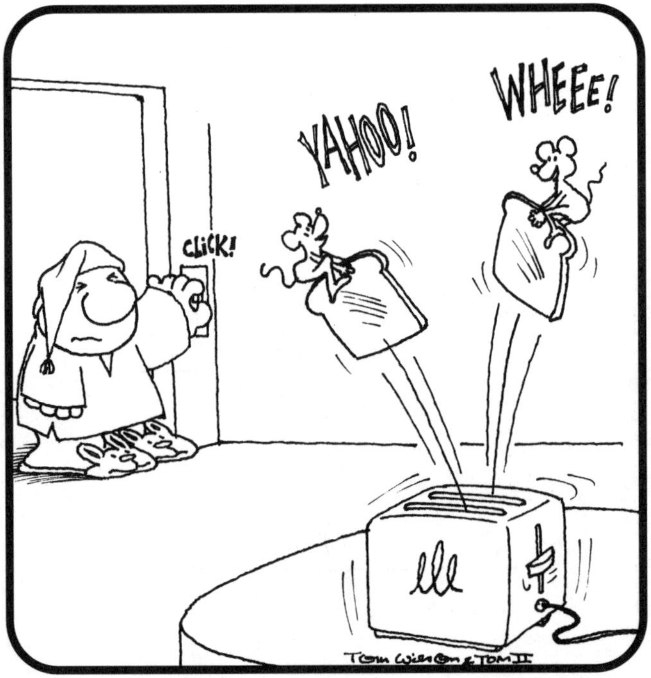
YAHOO!
WHEEE!
CLICK!
TOM WILSON & TOM II

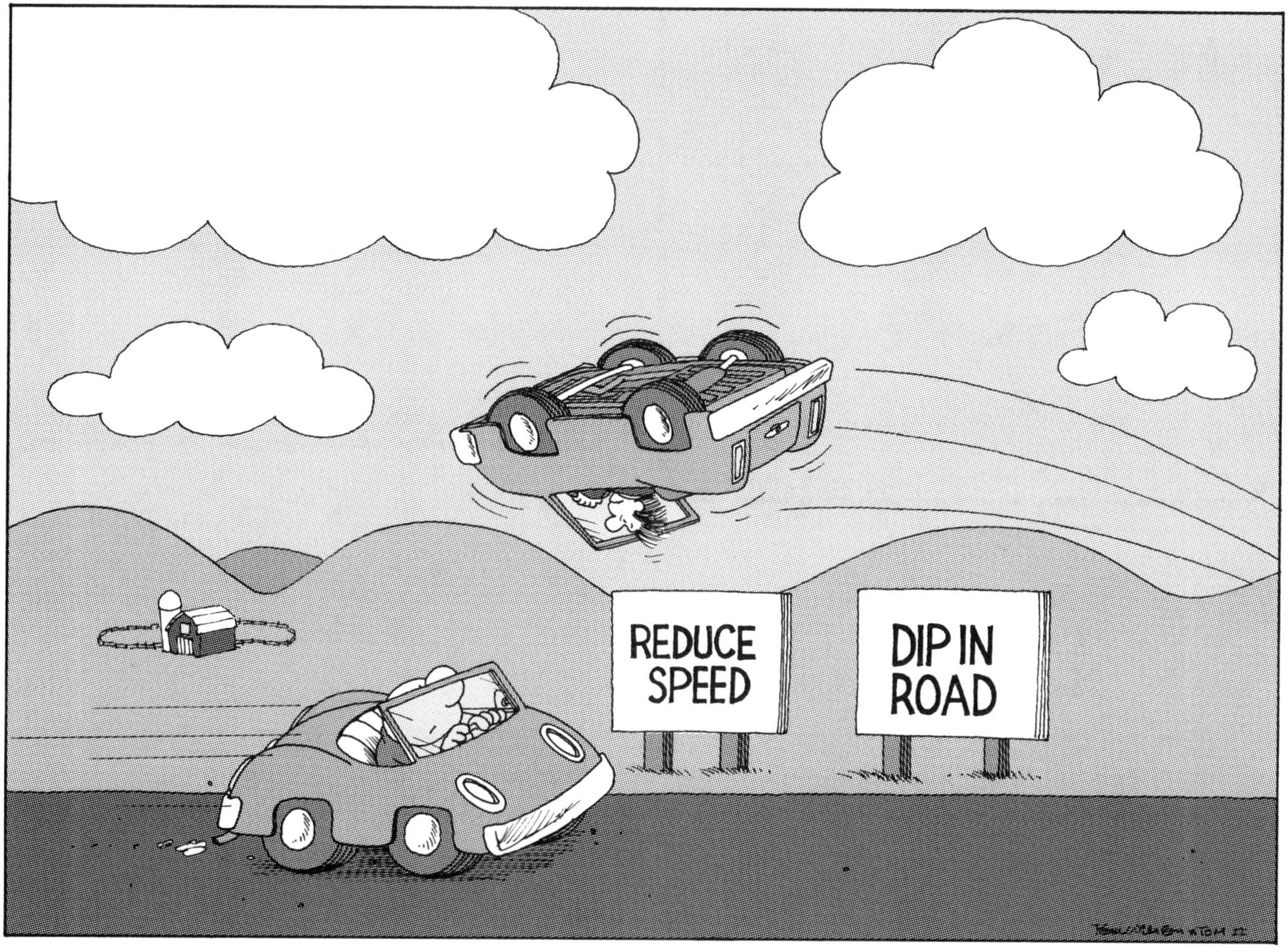
REDUCE
SPEED
DIP IN
ROAD

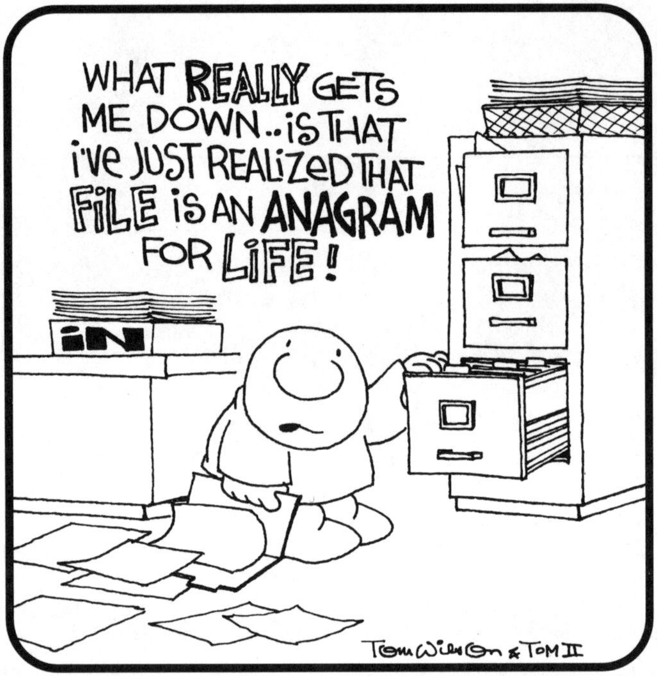
WHAT REALLY GETS ME DOWN.. IS THAT I'VE JUST REALIZED THAT FILE IS AN ANAGRAM FOR LIFE!
IN
TOM WILSON & TOM II

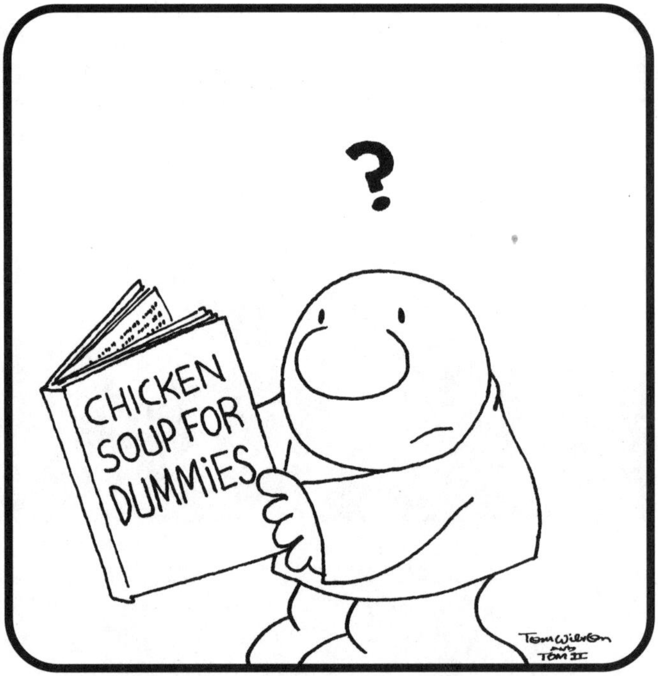
?
CHICKEN SOUP FOR DUMMIES
TOM WILSON AND TOM II

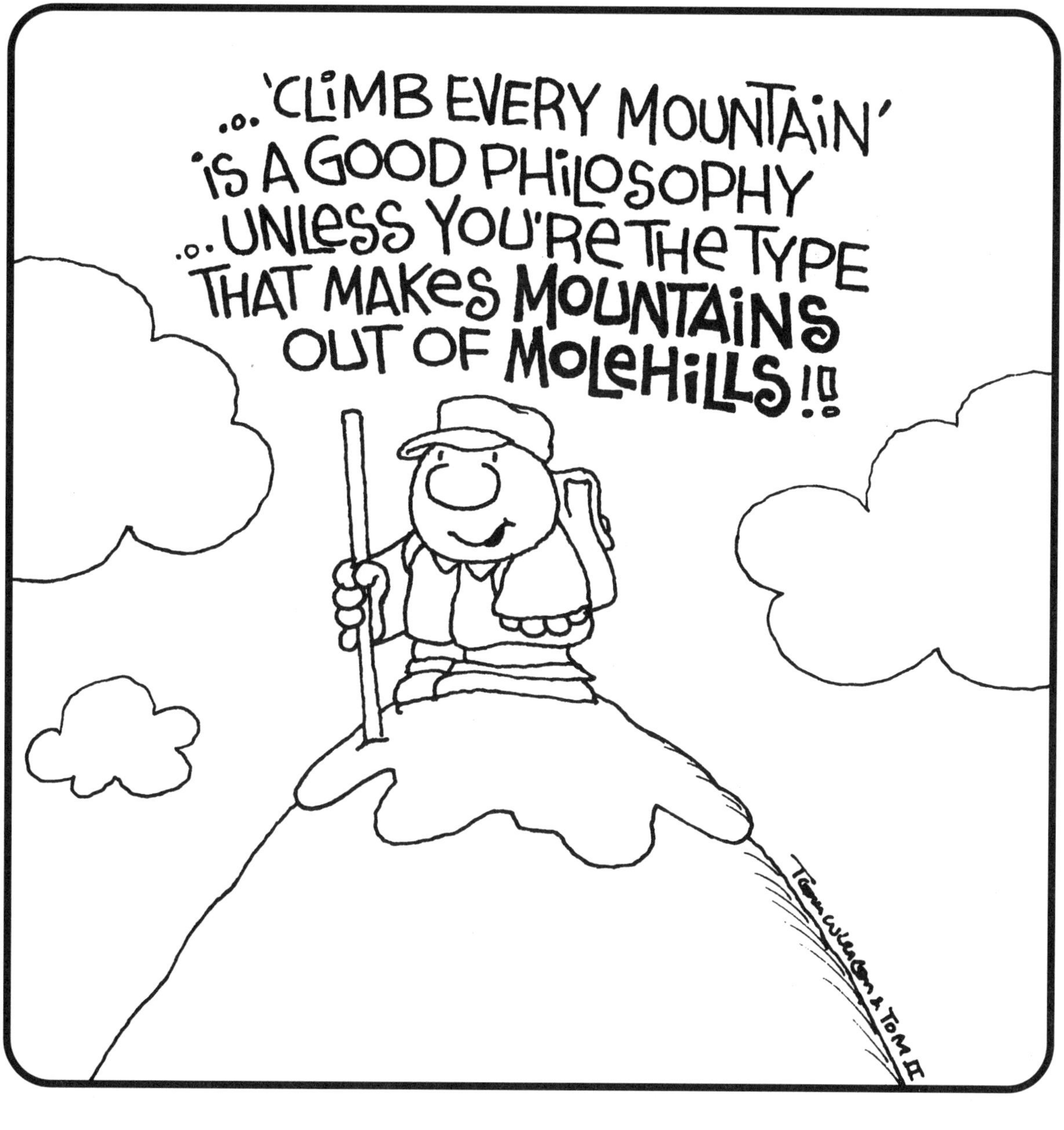
..o.. 'CLIMB EVERY MOUNTAIN' IS A GOOD PHILOSOPHY ..o.. UNLESS YOU'RE THE TYPE THAT MAKES MOUNTAINS OUT OF MOLEHILLS!!

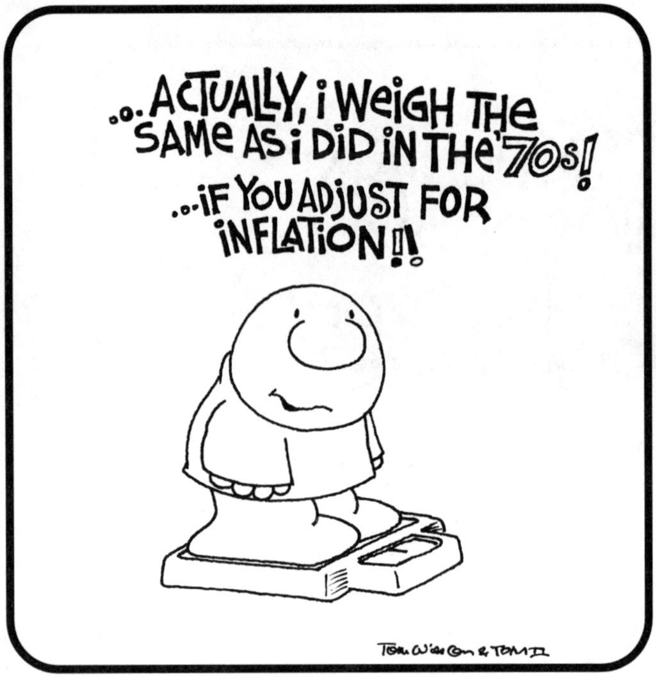
..o..ACTUALLY, i WEIGH THE SAME AS i DID IN THE '70S!
..o..iF YOU ADJUST FOR iNFLATION!!
TOM WILSON & TOM II

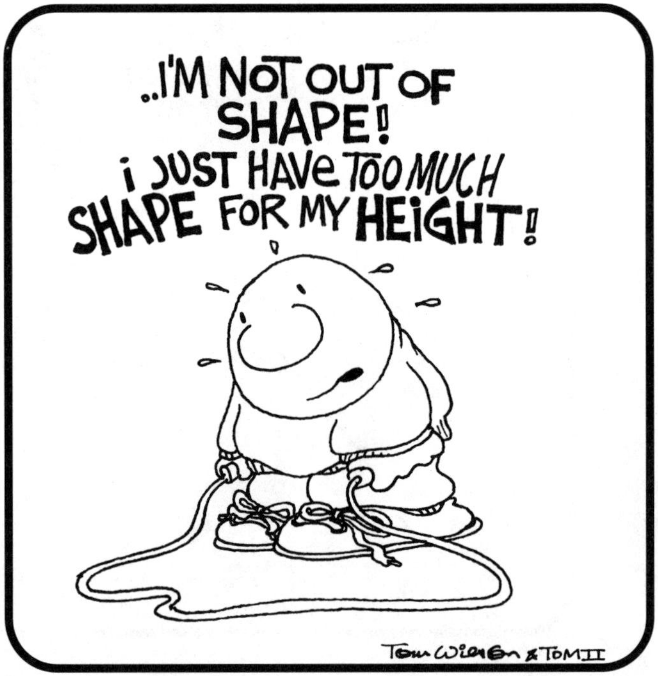
..I'M NOT OUT OF SHAPE!
i JUST HAVE TOO MUCH SHAPE FOR MY HEIGHT!
TOM WILSON & TOM II

THINGS TO DO TODAY:
DO THE LAUNDRY
MOP THE FLOOR
CLIP NOSE HAIR
DARN SOX
CLEAN TOILETS
WAX
SOMETIMES, I FEEL LIKE MY LIFE IS MUCH TO DO ABOUT NOTHING!
THINGS TO DO TODAY:
1. CLEAN LINT IN DRYER
2. TAKE OUT GARBAGE
3. DO THE LAUNDRY
4. MOP THE FLOOR
5. SCRUB THE KITCHEN
6. WASH THE WINDOWS
7. CLEAN THE CAR
8. CLEAN OUT CLOSET
9. CLIP NOSE HAIR
10. POLISH TOENAIL CLIPPERS
11. DARN SOXS
12. STRAIGHTEN PAPER CLIPS
13. CLEAN TOILETS
14. RE-GROUT SHOWER

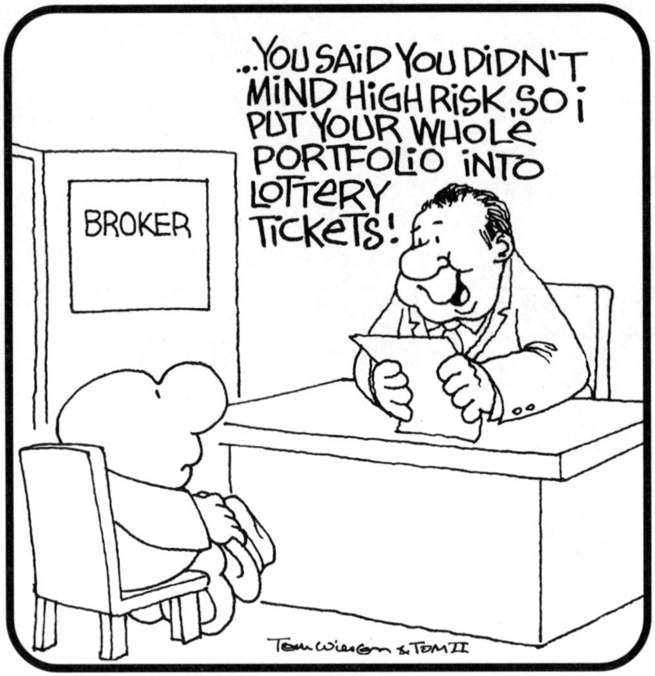
...YOU SAID YOU DIDN'T MIND HIGH RISK, SO I PUT YOUR WHOLE PORTFOLIO INTO LOTTERY TICKETS!
BROKER
TOM WILSON & TOM II

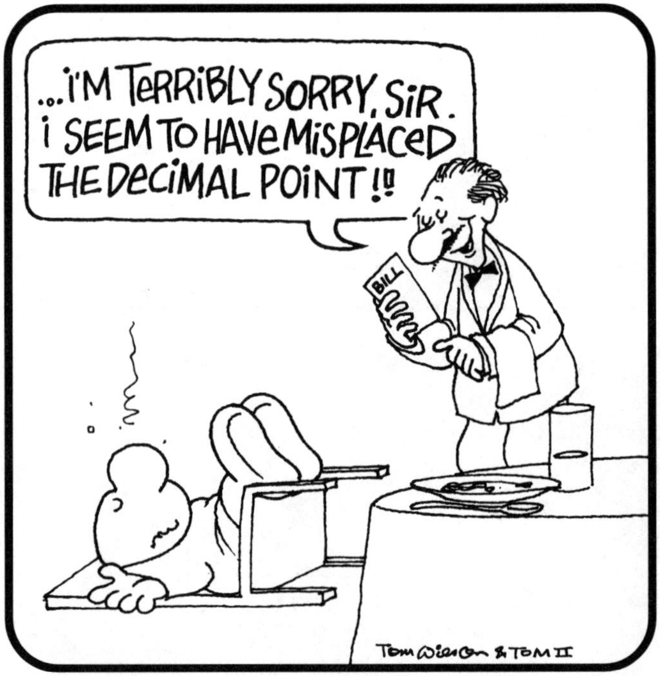
...I'M TERRIBLY SORRY, SIR. I SEEM TO HAVE MISPLACED THE DECIMAL POINT!!
BILL
TOM WILSON & TOM II

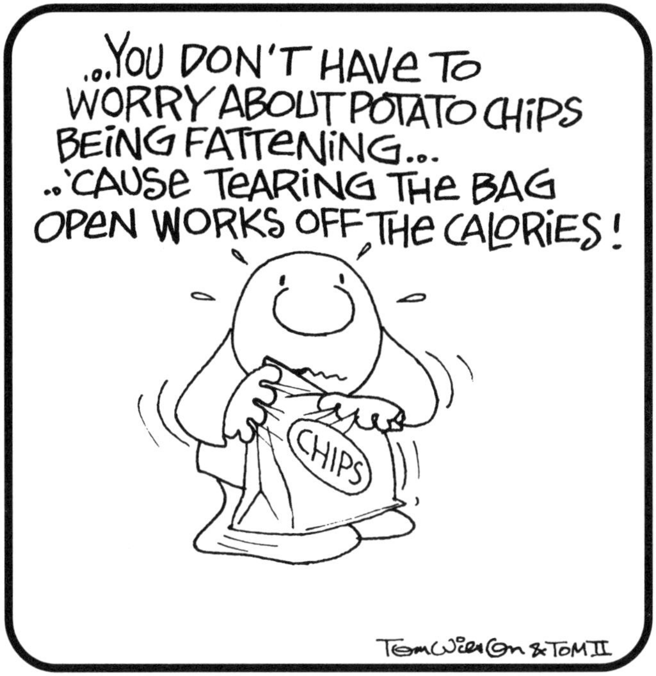
..YOU DON'T HAVE TO WORRY ABOUT POTATO CHIPS BEING FATTENING...
..'CAUSE TEARING THE BAG OPEN WORKS OFF THE CALORIES!
CHIPS
TOM WILSON & TOM II

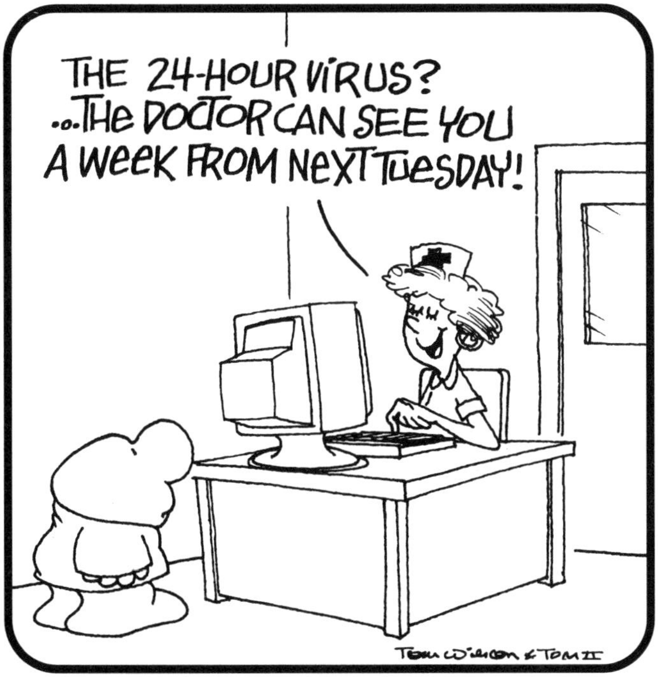
THE 24-HOUR VIRUS?
..THE DOCTOR CAN SEE YOU A WEEK FROM NEXT TUESDAY!
TOM WILSON & TOM II

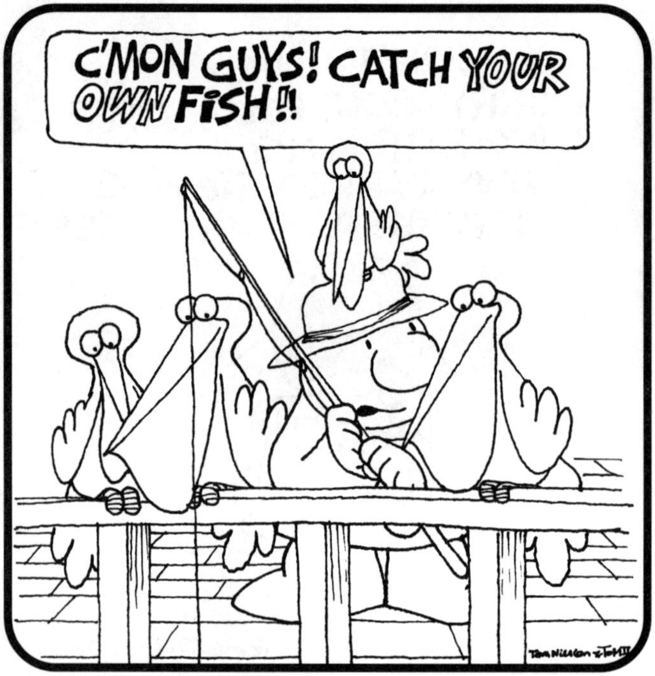
C'MON GUYS! CATCH YOUR OWN FISH!!
TOM WILSON & TOM II

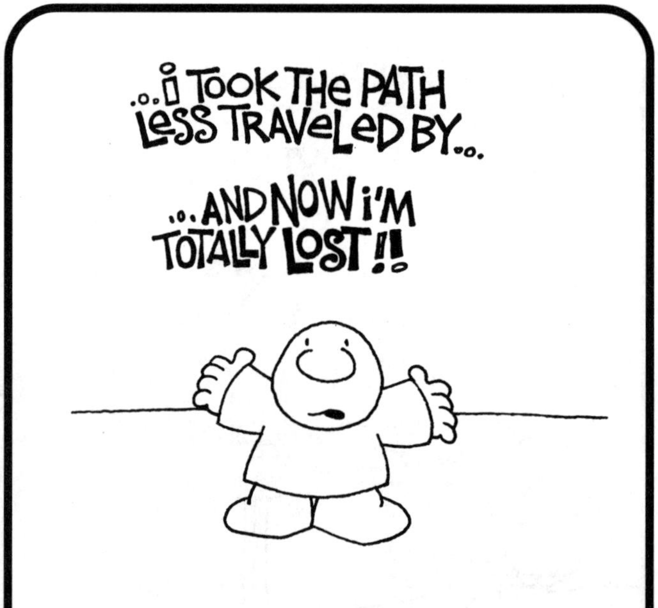
...I TOOK THE PATH LESS TRAVELED BY...
...AND NOW I'M TOTALLY LOST!!
TOM WILSON & TOM II

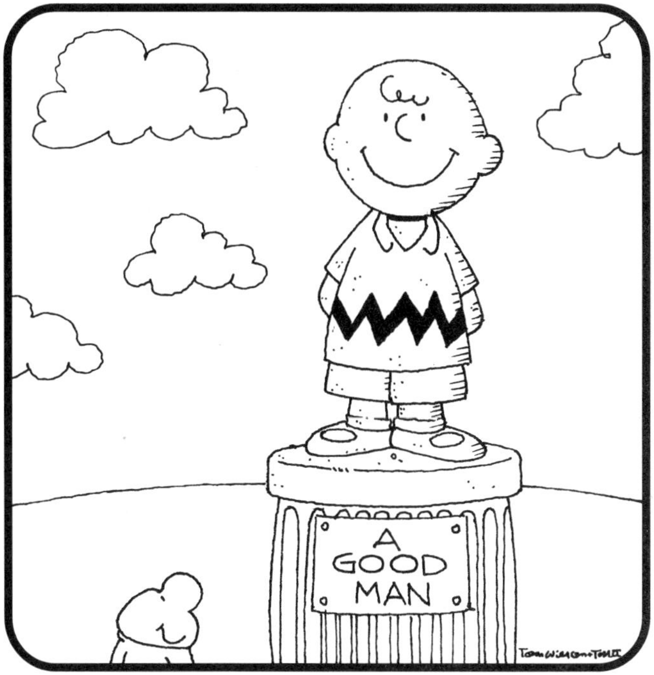
A
GOOD
MAN
Tom Wilson & Tom II

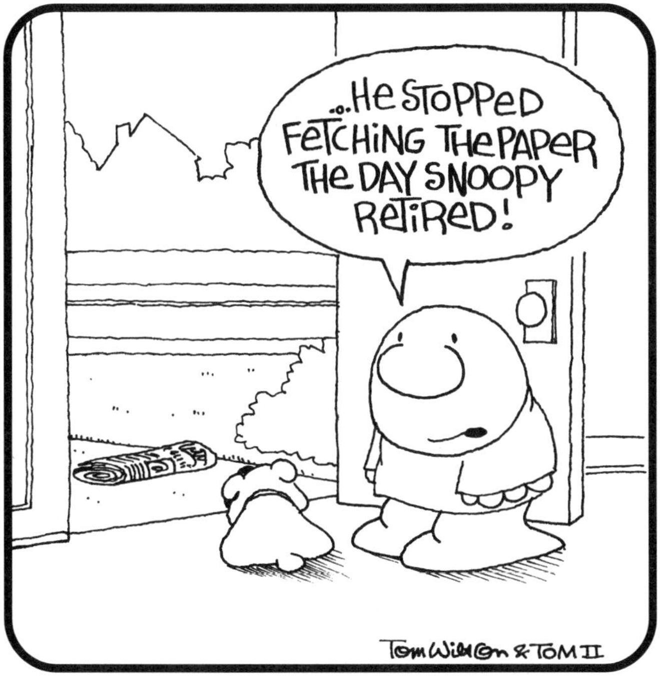
...HE STOPPED FETCHING THE PAPER THE DAY SNOOPY RETIRED!
Tom Wilson & TOM II

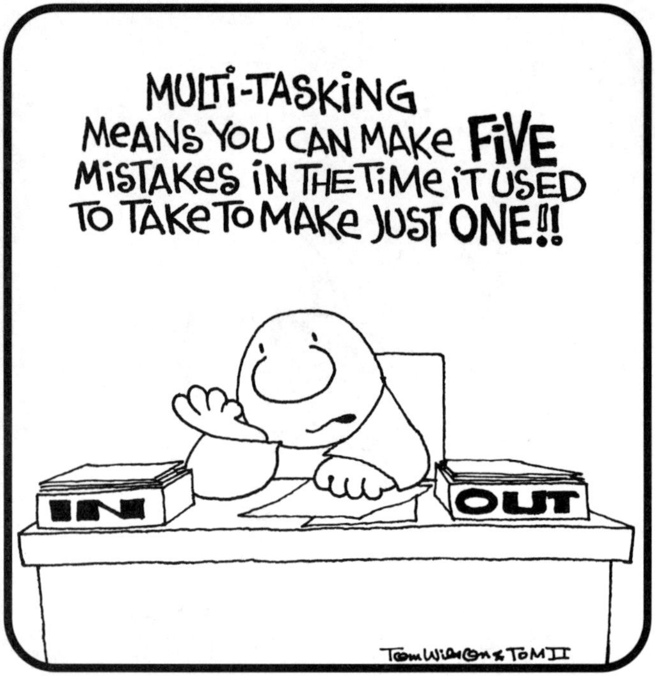
MULTI-TASKING MEANS YOU CAN MAKE FIVE MISTAKES IN THE TIME IT USED TO TAKE TO MAKE JUST ONE!!
IN
OUT
Tom Wilson & Tom II

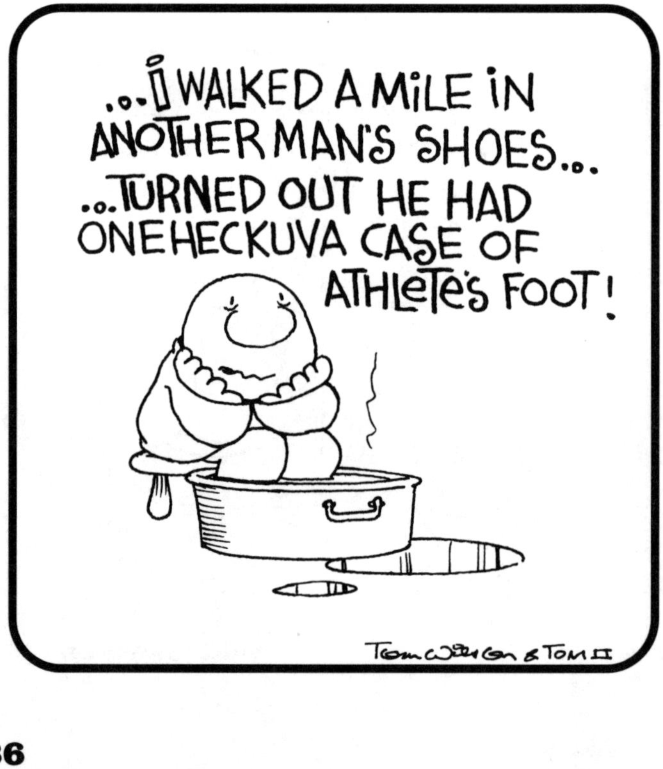
...I WALKED A MILE IN ANOTHER MAN'S SHOES... ...TURNED OUT HE HAD ONE HECKUVA CASE OF ATHLETE'S FOOT!
Tom Wilson & Tom II

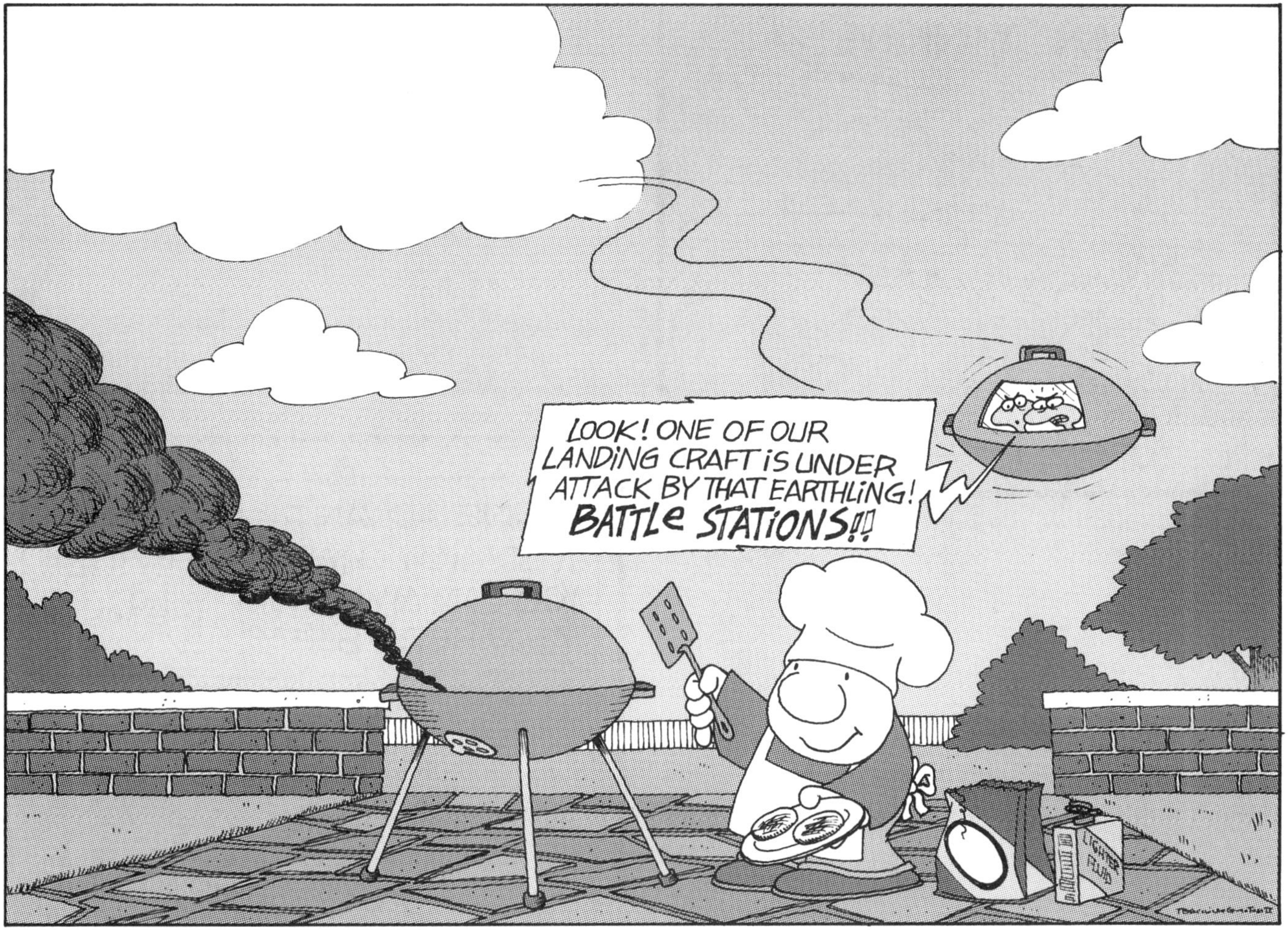
LOOK! ONE OF OUR LANDING CRAFT IS UNDER ATTACK BY THAT EARTHLING! BATTLE STATIONS!!
LIGHTER FLUID

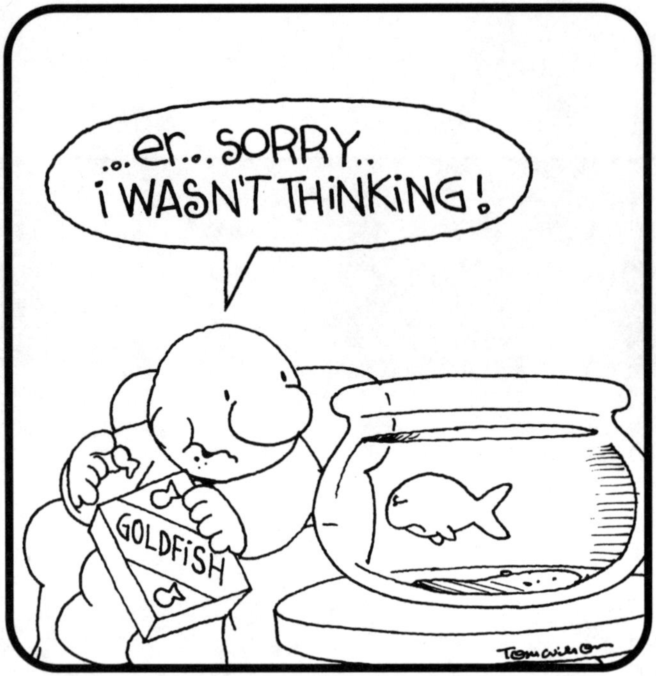
..er...SORRY..
i WASN'T THiNKiNG!
GOLDFiSH

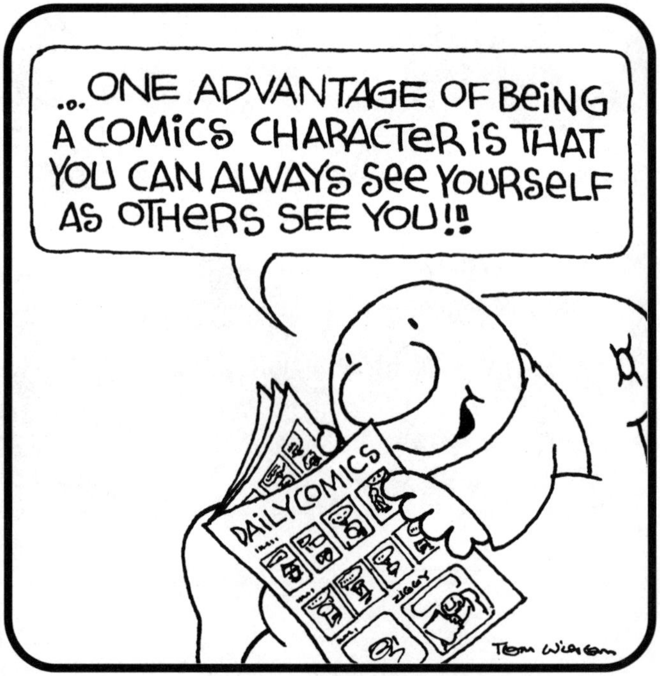
..ONE ADVANTAGE OF BeiNG A COMiCS CHARACTeR iS THAT YOU CAN ALWAYS See YOURSeLF AS OTHeRS SEE YOU!!
DAiLY COMiCS
ZiGGY

BUILD IT AND THEY WILL COME!
BUILD IT AND THEY WILL COME!
BUILD IT AND THEY WILL COME!
BUILD IT AND THEY WILL COME!
..I MUST BUILD IT AND THEY WILL COME!
..BUILD IT AND THEY WILL COME!
..I MUST BUILD IT!
THIS SURE SEEMS LIKE ..A LOT OF TROUBLE TO GO THROUGH JUST TO GET A NEW BIRD-FEEDER!!

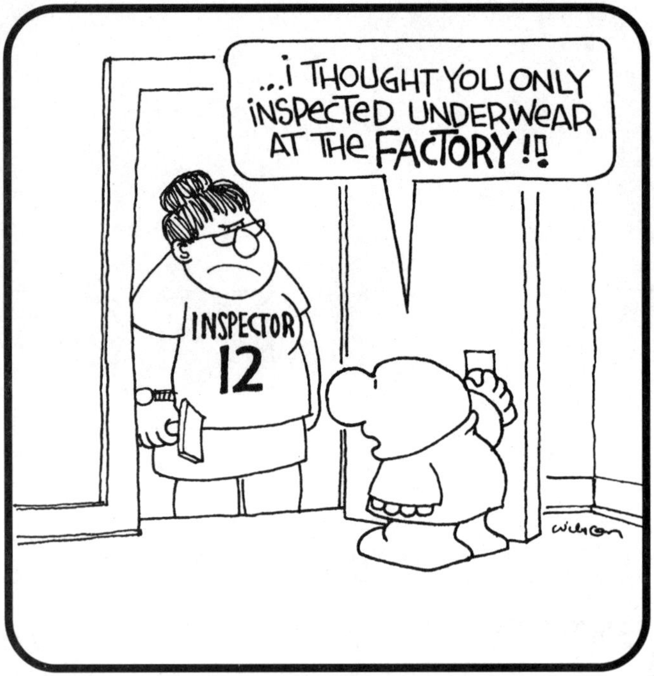

...I THOUGHT YOU ONLY INSPECTED UNDERWEAR AT THE FACTORY!!
INSPECTOR 12

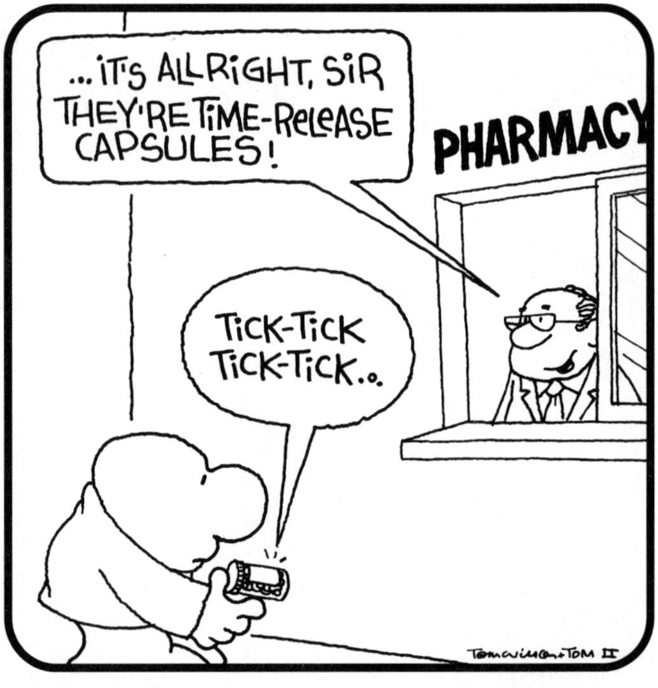

...IT'S ALLRIGHT, SIR THEY'RE TIME-RELEASE CAPSULES!
PHARMACY
TICK-TICK TICK-TICK...

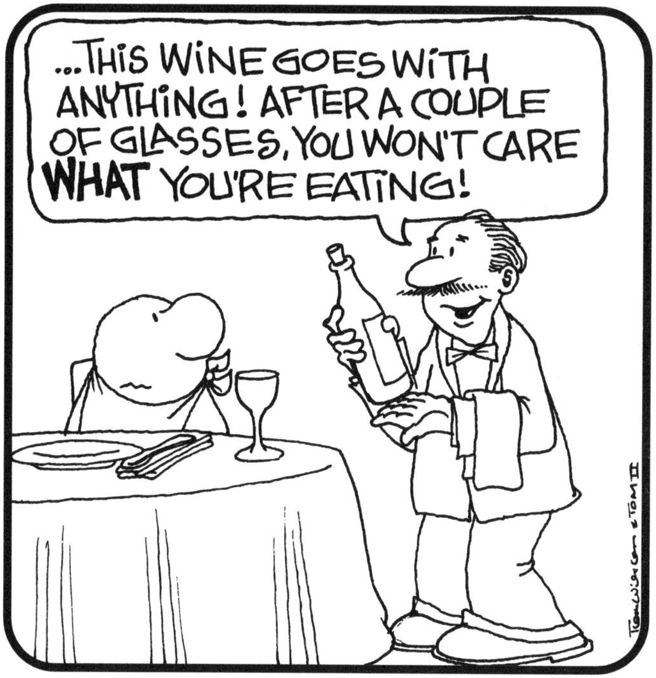
...THIS WINE GOES WITH ANYTHING! AFTER A COUPLE OF GLASSES, YOU WON'T CARE WHAT YOU'RE EATING!

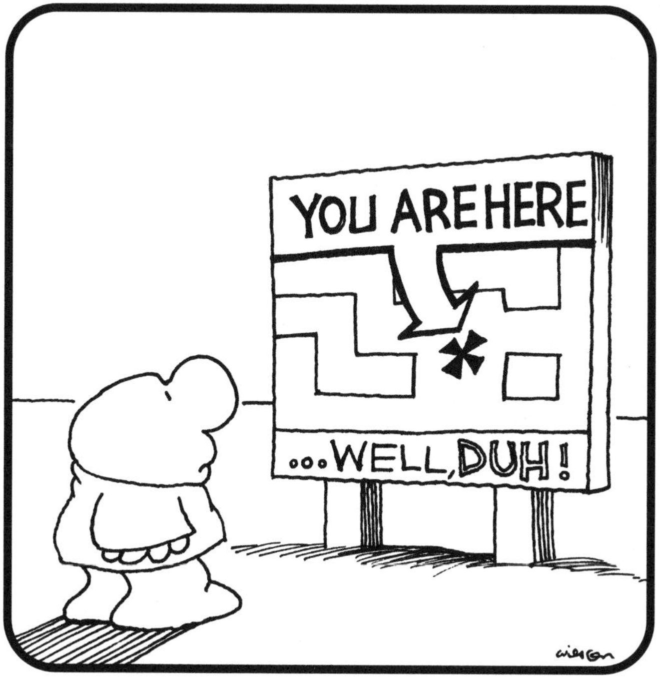
YOU ARE HERE
...WELL, DUH!

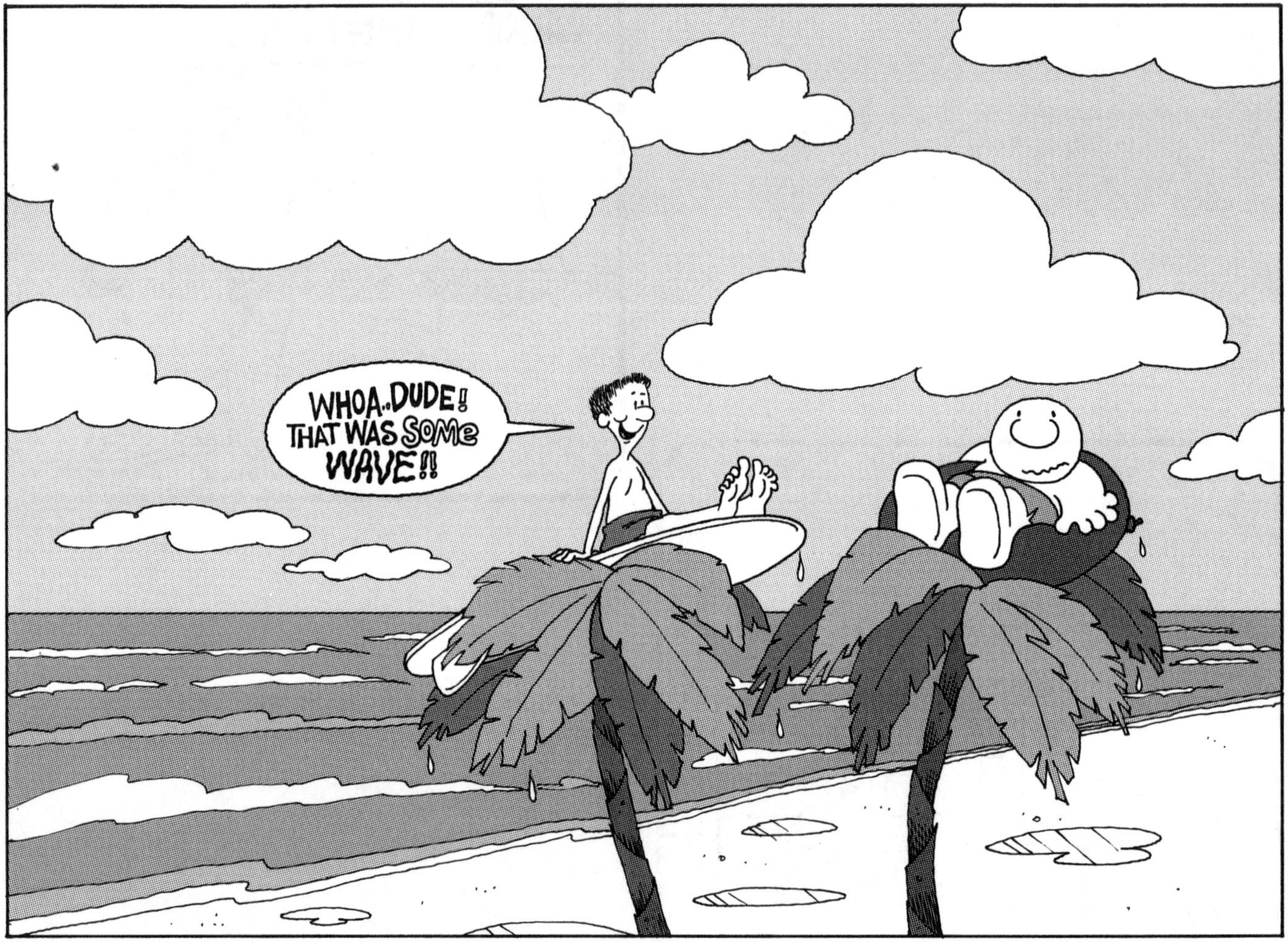
WHOA..DUDE! THAT WAS SOME WAVE!!

SNORe
SNORE.o.
..SNORKA..
SNURG
SNORe..
SNORe.o.
SNURK..
SNURKA
SNORRK
SNORK
BONK!!
?

...IT'S A COMMON PROBLEM. MOST CARTOON CHARACTERS DON'T HAVE DEPTH PERCEPTION!
E
TOM WILSON & TOM II

PHARMACY
...THIS PRESCRIPTION IS AWFULLY EASY TO READ—ARE YOU SURE THIS GUY IS A REAL DOCTOR?
TOM WILSON & TOM II

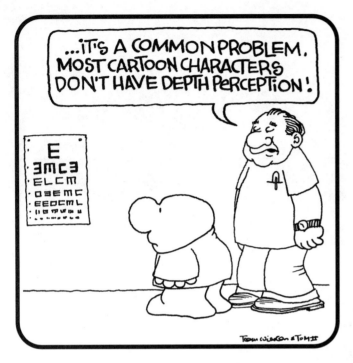

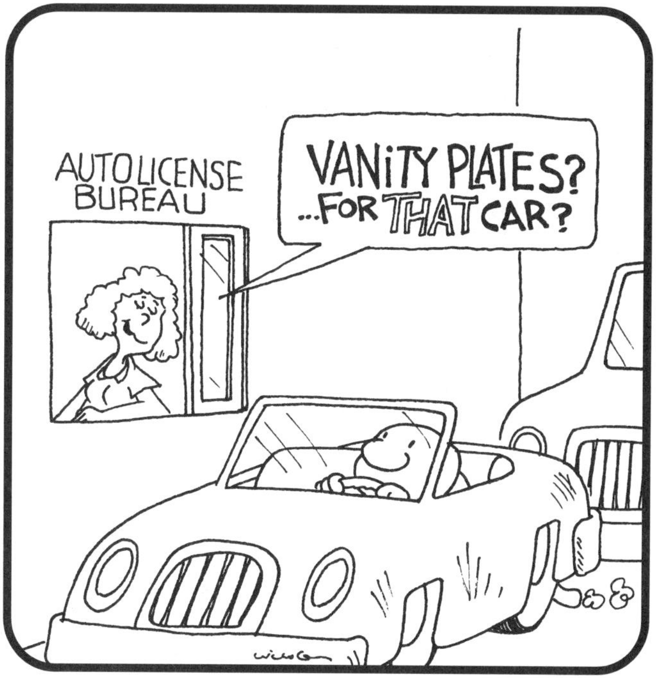
AUTO LICENSE BUREAU
VANITY PLATES? ...FOR THAT CAR?

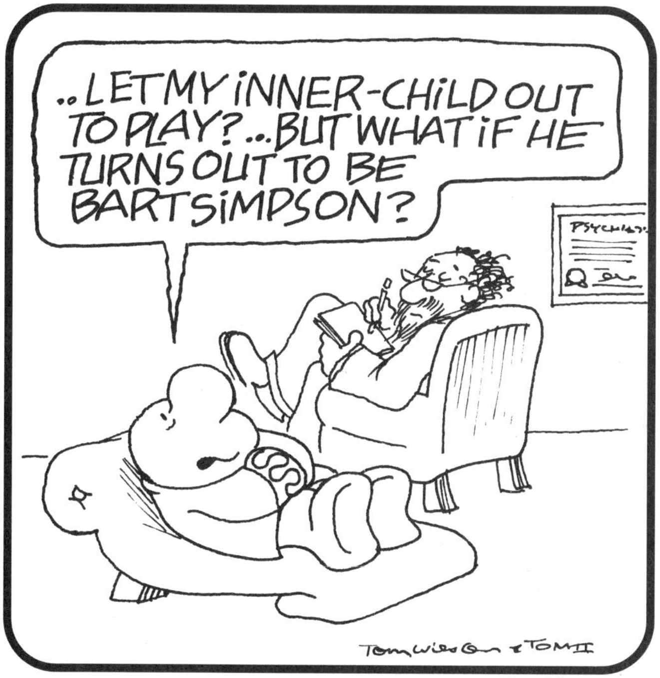
..LET MY INNER-CHILD OUT TO PLAY? ...BUT WHAT IF HE TURNS OUT TO BE BART SIMPSON?

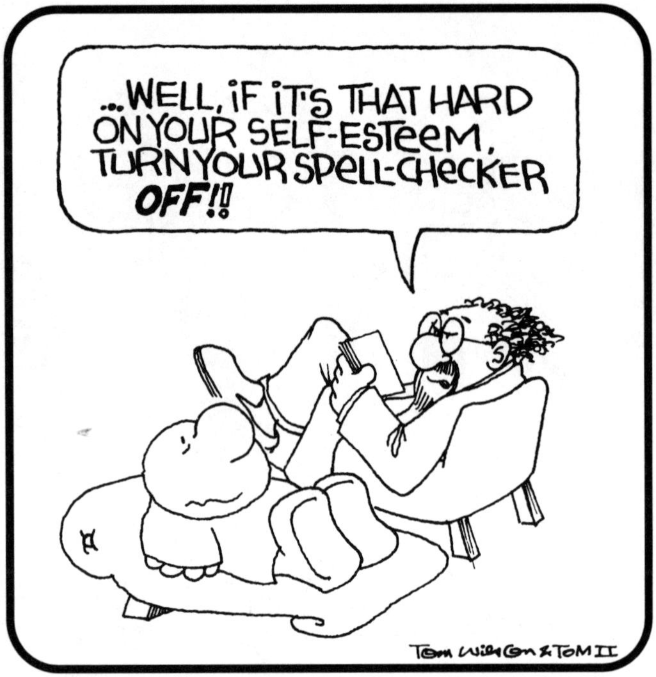

...WELL, IF IT'S THAT HARD ON YOUR SELF-ESTEEM, TURN YOUR SPELL-CHECKER OFF!!
TOM WILSON & TOM II

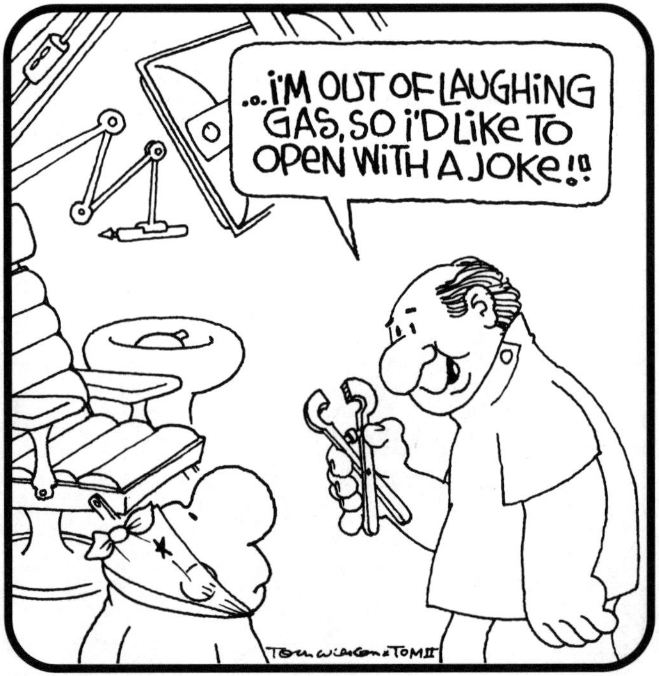

...I'M OUT OF LAUGHING GAS, SO I'D LIKE TO OPEN WITH A JOKE!!
TOM WILSON & TOM II

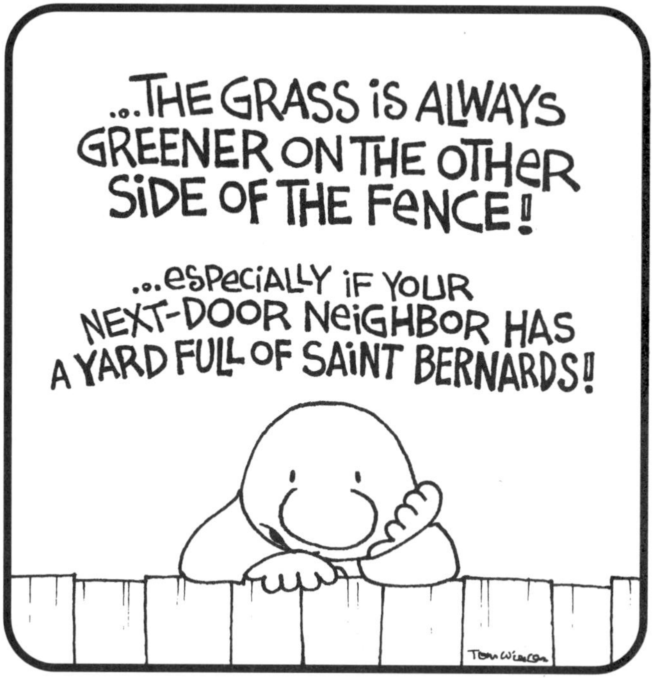
...THE GRASS IS ALWAYS GREENER ON THE OTHER SIDE OF THE FENCE!
...ESPECIALLY IF YOUR NEXT-DOOR NEIGHBOR HAS A YARD FULL OF SAINT BERNARDS!

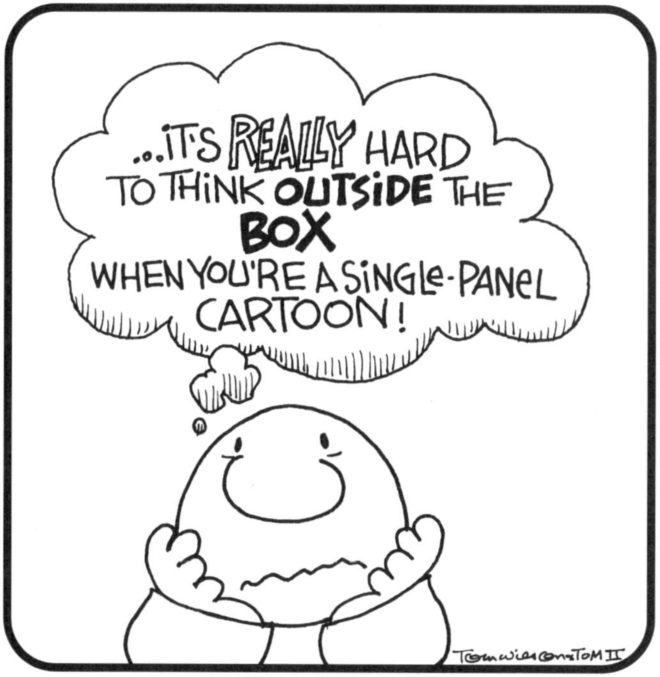
...IT'S REALLY HARD TO THINK OUTSIDE THE BOX WHEN YOU'RE A SINGLE-PANEL CARTOON!

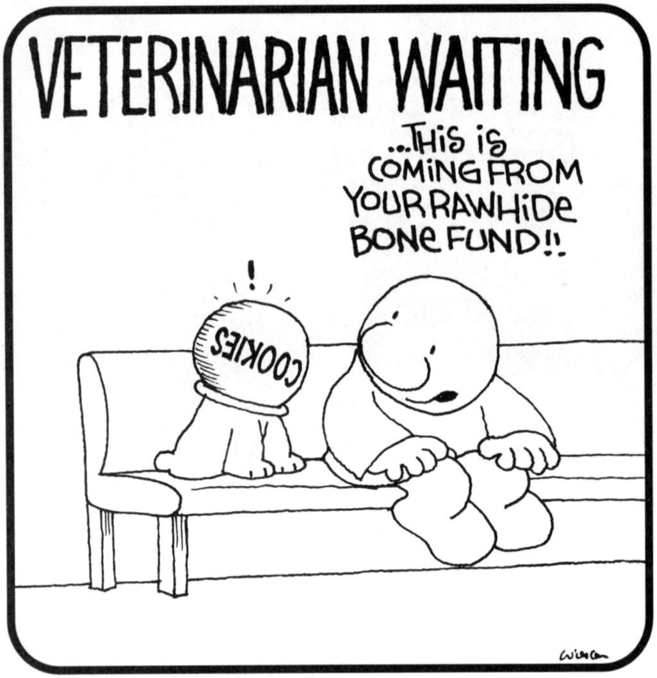
VETERINARIAN WAITING
...THIS is COMING FROM YOUR RAWHIDE BONE FUND!!
!
COOKIES

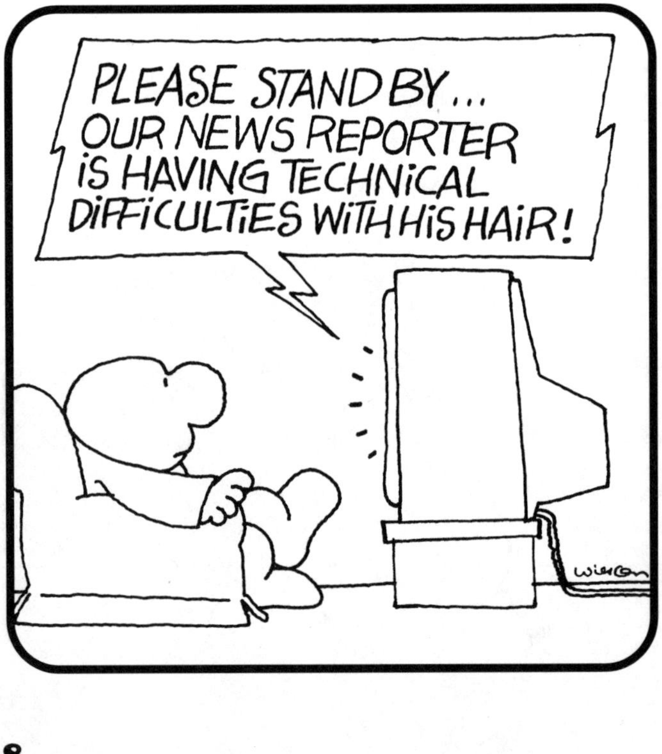
PLEASE STAND BY... OUR NEWS REPORTER IS HAVING TECHNICAL DIFFICULTIES WITH HIS HAIR!

..WHAT DO YOU RECOMMEND, HENRI?
MENU
WELL, TODAY OUR SPECIAL IS CHICKEN...
...ON A BED OF WILD RICE WITH GREEN BEANS ALMONDINE AND A NICE SIDE SALAD!
MENU
..WITH A SUCCULENT SHRIMP COCKTAIL AND YOUR CHOICE OF BEVERAGE AND DESSERT.
THAT SOUNDS GREAT!..HOW IS THE CHICKEN PREPARED?
MENU
..WE BREAK IT TO HIM VERY GENTLY AND TELL HIM IT'S NOTHING PERSONAL!

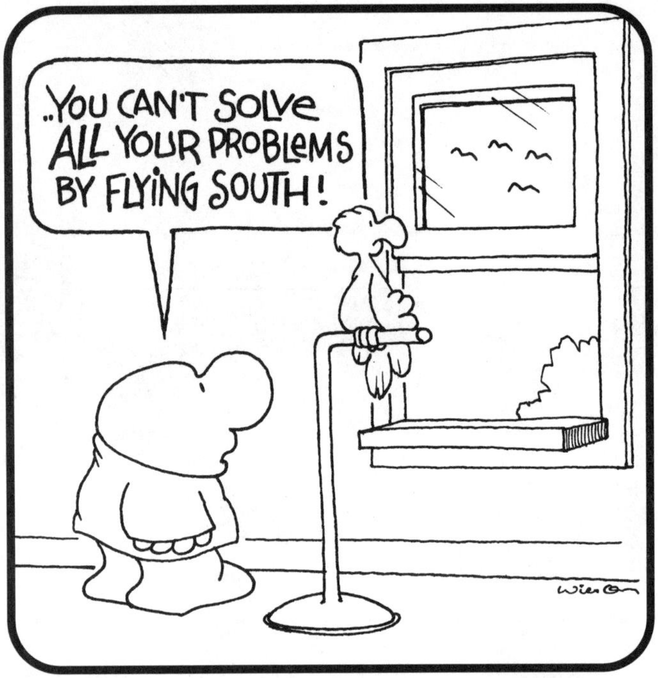
..YOU CAN'T SOLVE ALL YOUR PROBLEMS BY FLYING SOUTH!

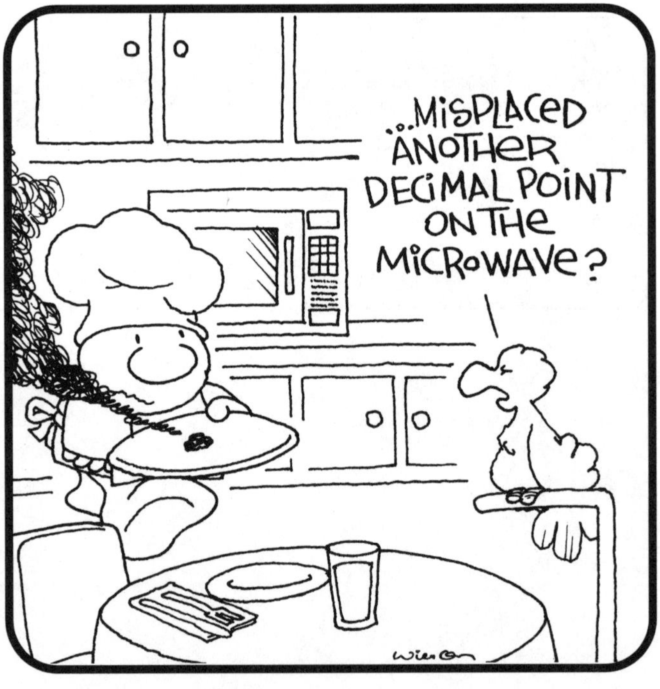
...MISPLACED ANOTHER DECIMAL POINT ON THE MICROWAVE?

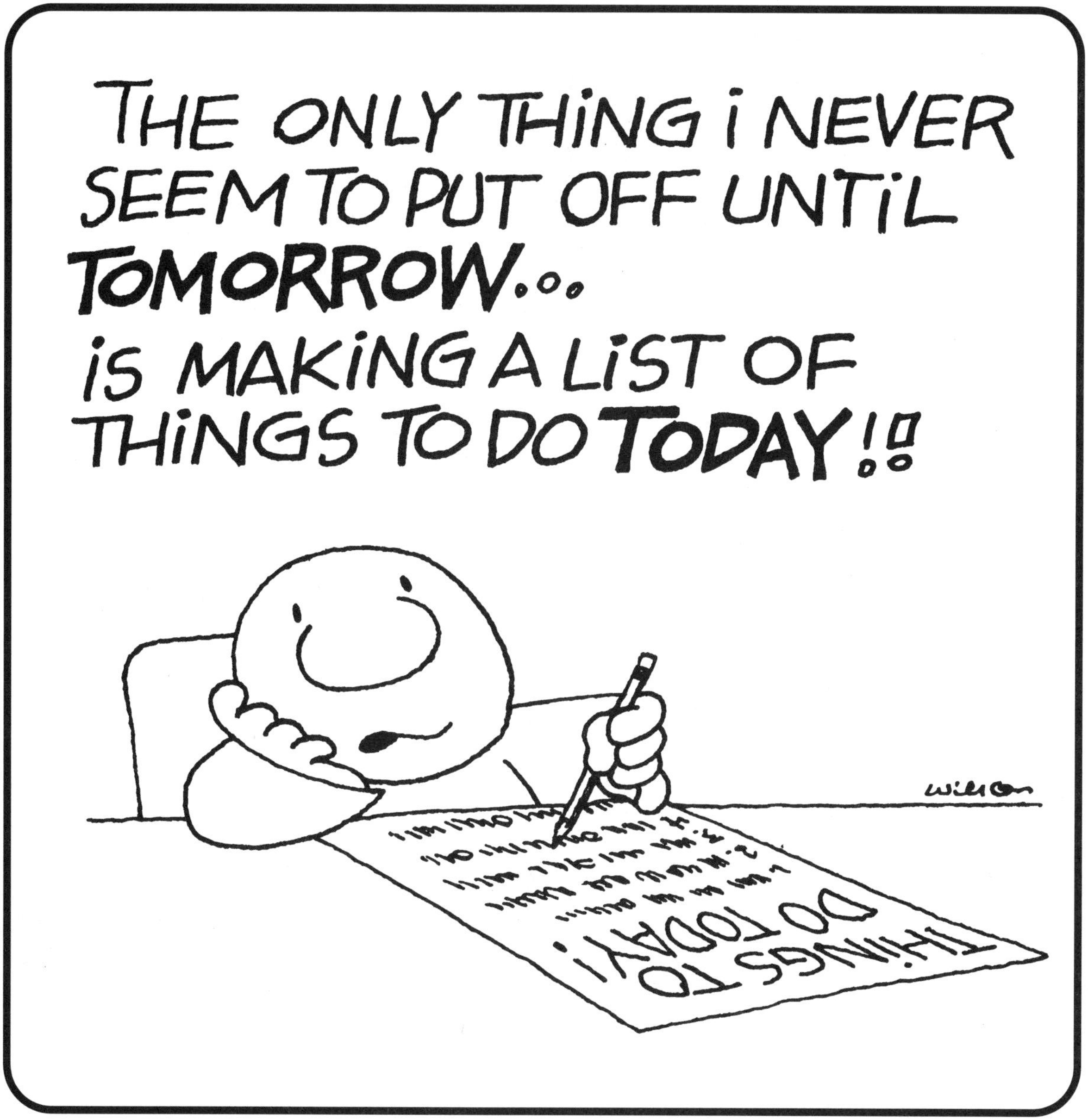
THE ONLY THING I NEVER SEEM TO PUT OFF UNTIL TOMORROW... IS MAKING A LIST OF THINGS TO DO TODAY!!
THINGS TO DO TODAY!
WILSON

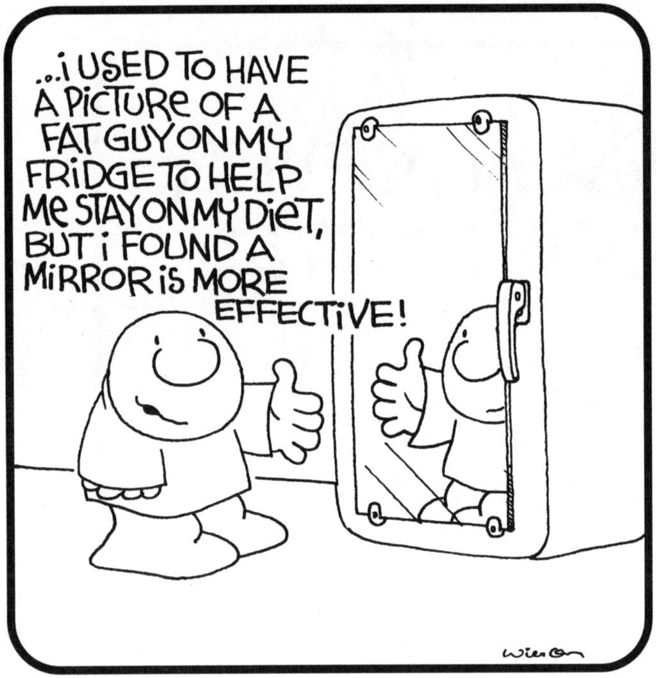
...i USED TO HAVE A PICTURE OF A FAT GUY ON MY FRIDGE TO HELP ME STAY ON MY DIET, BUT i FOUND A MIRROR iS MORE EFFECTIVE!

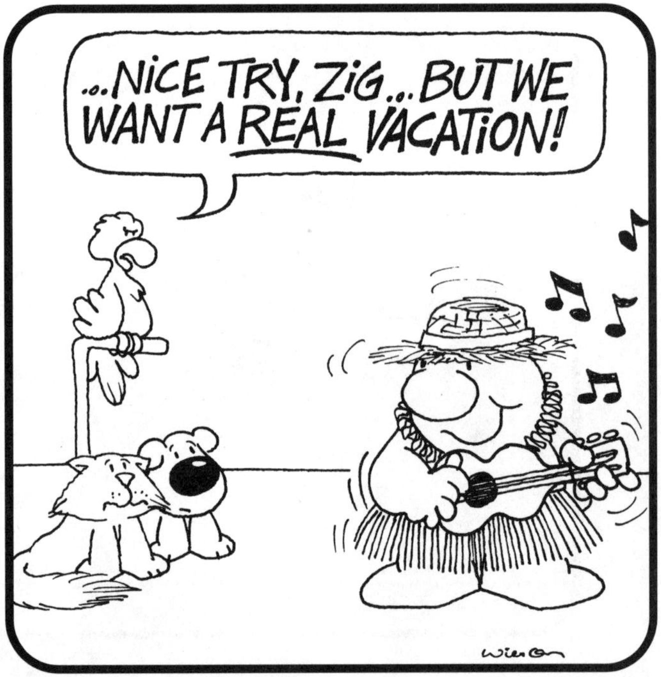
...NICE TRY, ZiG... BUT WE WANT A REAL VACATiON!

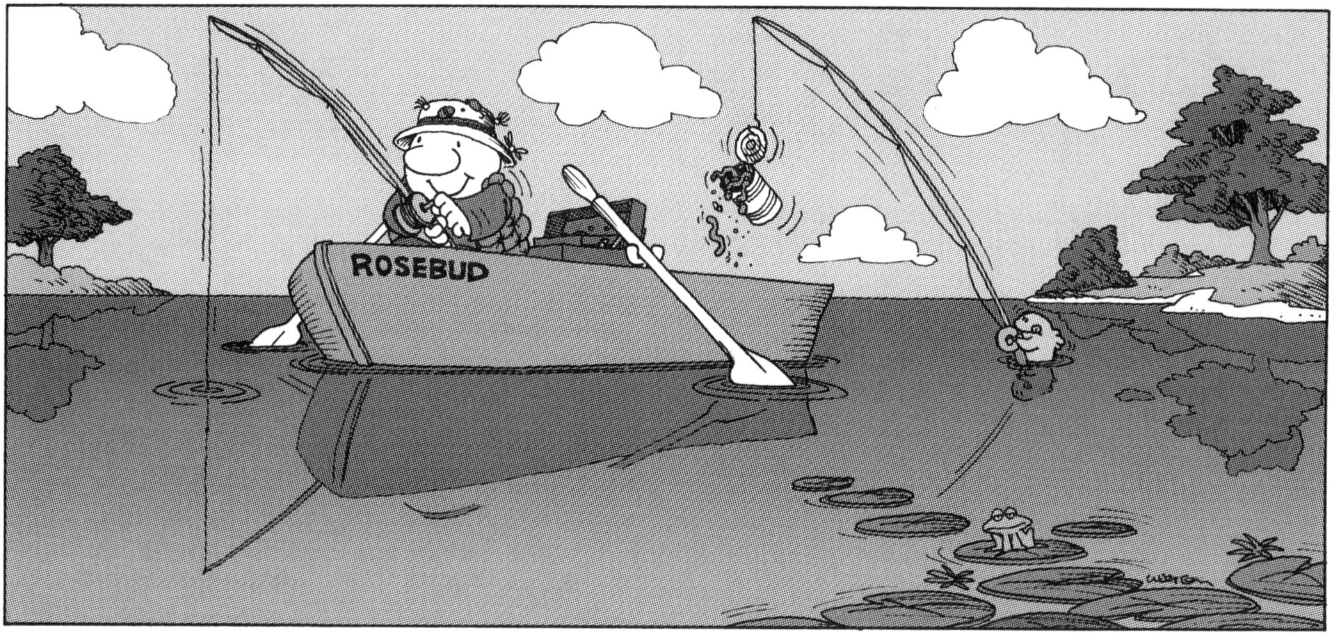
ROSEBUD

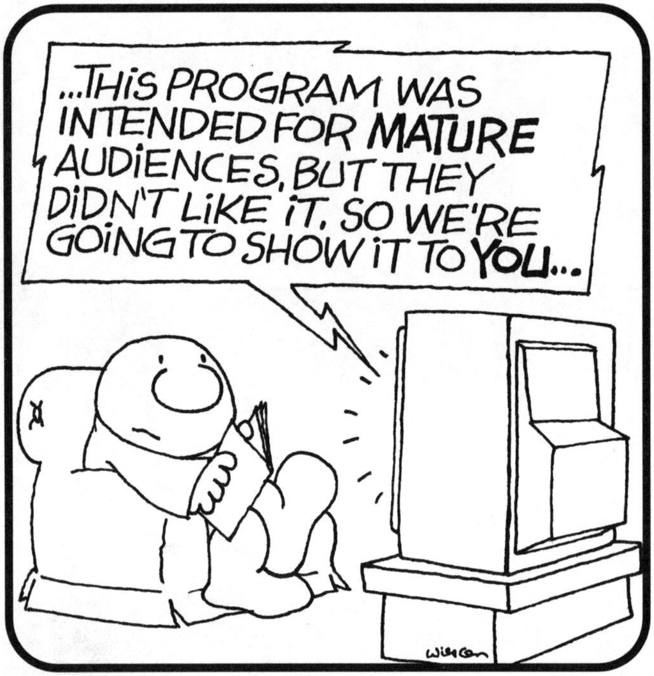
...THIS PROGRAM WAS INTENDED FOR MATURE AUDIENCES, BUT THEY DIDN'T LIKE IT, SO WE'RE GOING TO SHOW IT TO YOU...
Wilson

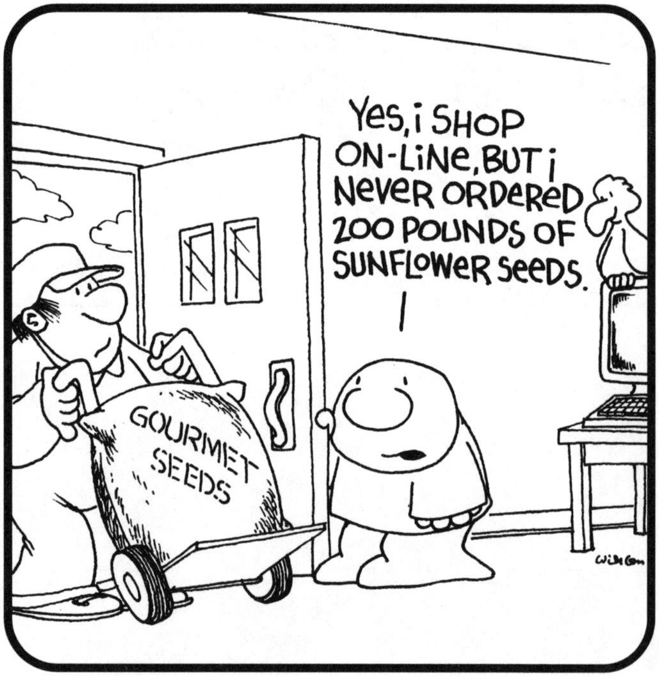
YES, I SHOP ON-LINE, BUT I NEVER ORDERED 200 POUNDS OF SUNFLOWER SEEDS.
GOURMET SEEDS
Wilson

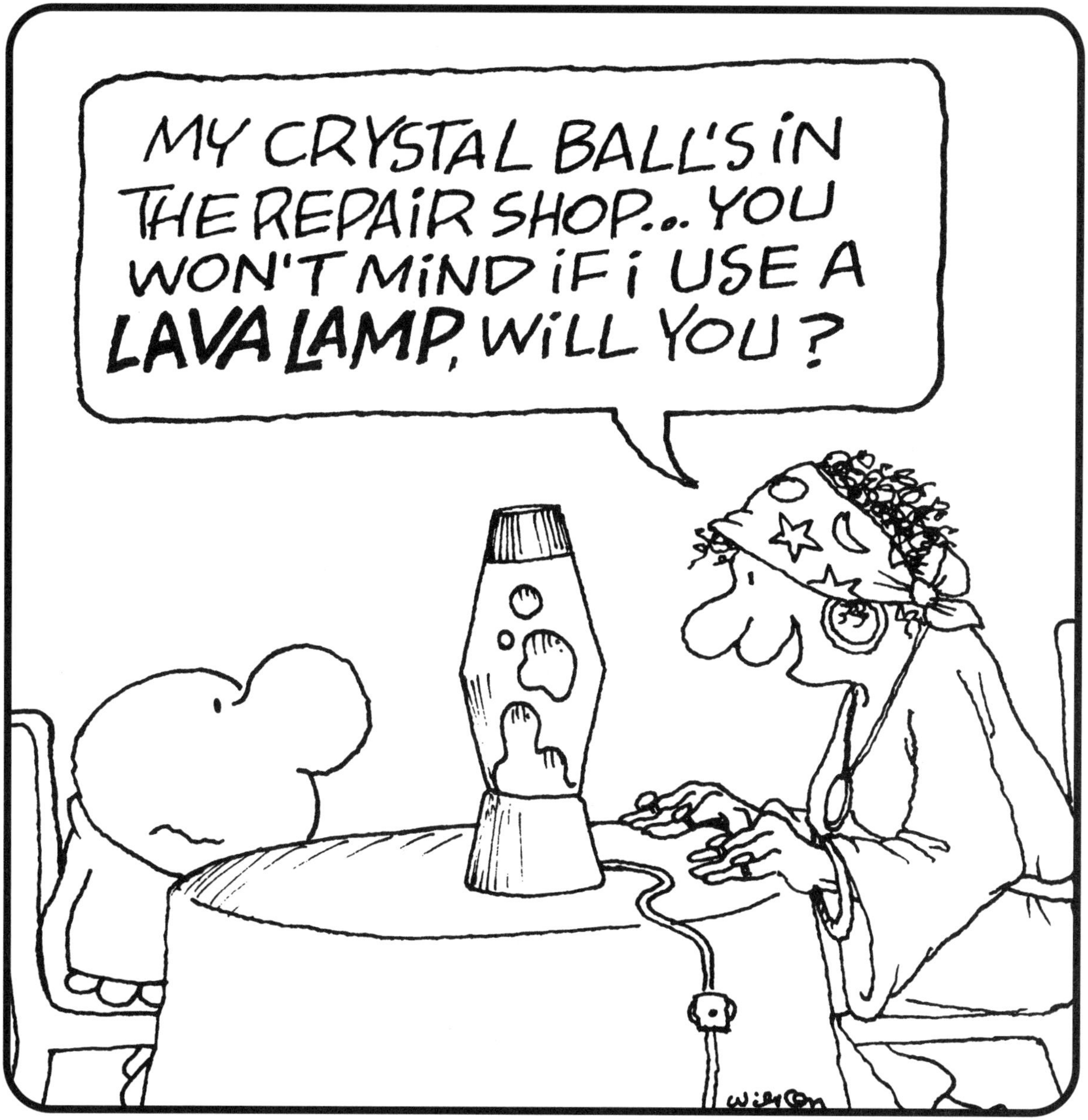
MY CRYSTAL BALL'S IN THE REPAIR SHOP... YOU WON'T MIND IF I USE A **LAVA LAMP**, WILL YOU?
WILSON

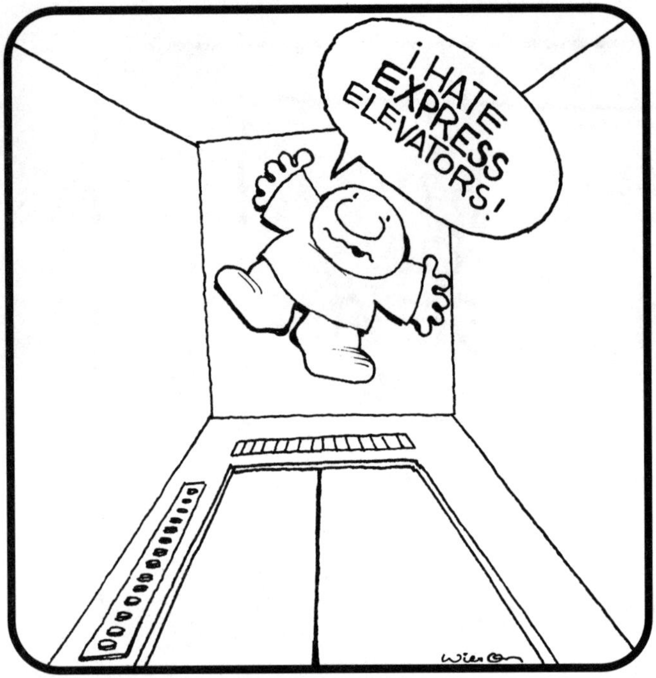
¡ HATE EXPRESS ELEVATORS!
Wilson

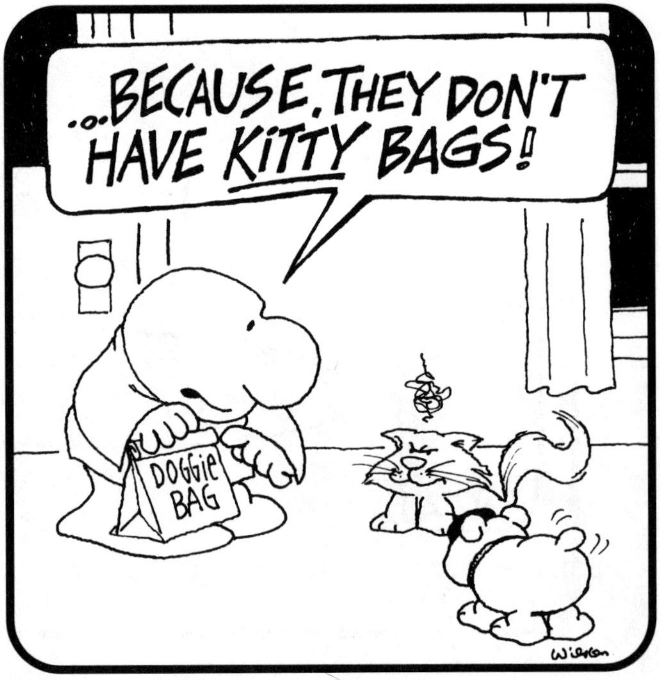
..o..BECAUSE, THEY DON'T HAVE KITTY BAGS!
DOGGIE BAG
Wilson

PRIZE PATROL
ZIGGY
PRIZE PATROL
ZIGGY
SCREECH!!
PRIZE PATROL
ZIGGY
ZIGGY
DING
DONG
HELLO, SIR .. ARE YOU THE HEAD OF THE HOUSEHOLD?
YES! YES I AM!
CONGRATULATIONS
..COULD YOU DIRECT US TO A MRS. EDNA MURPHY OF 301 ELM STREET?

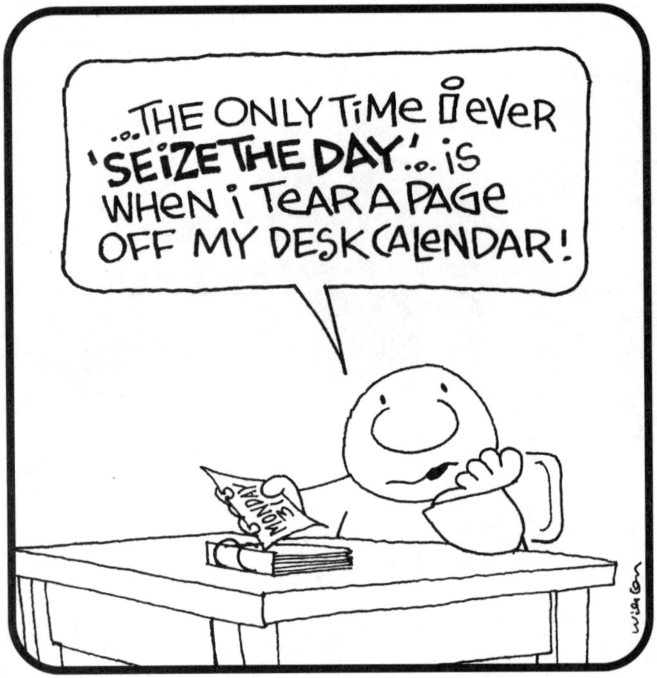
..THE ONLY TiMe i eVeR 'SEiZE THE DAY'.. iS WHeN i TeAR A PAGe OFF MY DESK CALeNDAR!
MONDAY 13

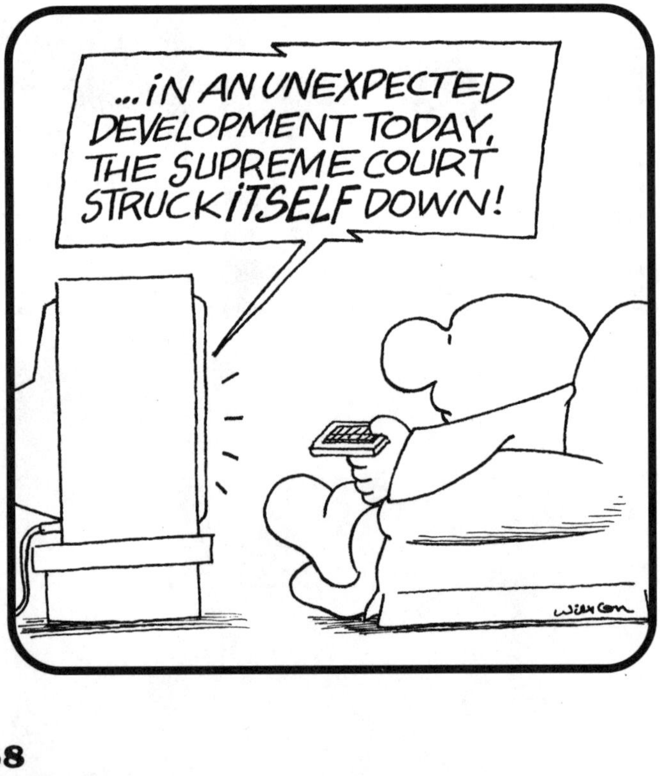
...iN AN UNEXPECTED DEVELOPMENT TODAY, THE SUPREME COURT STRUCK iTSELF DOWN!

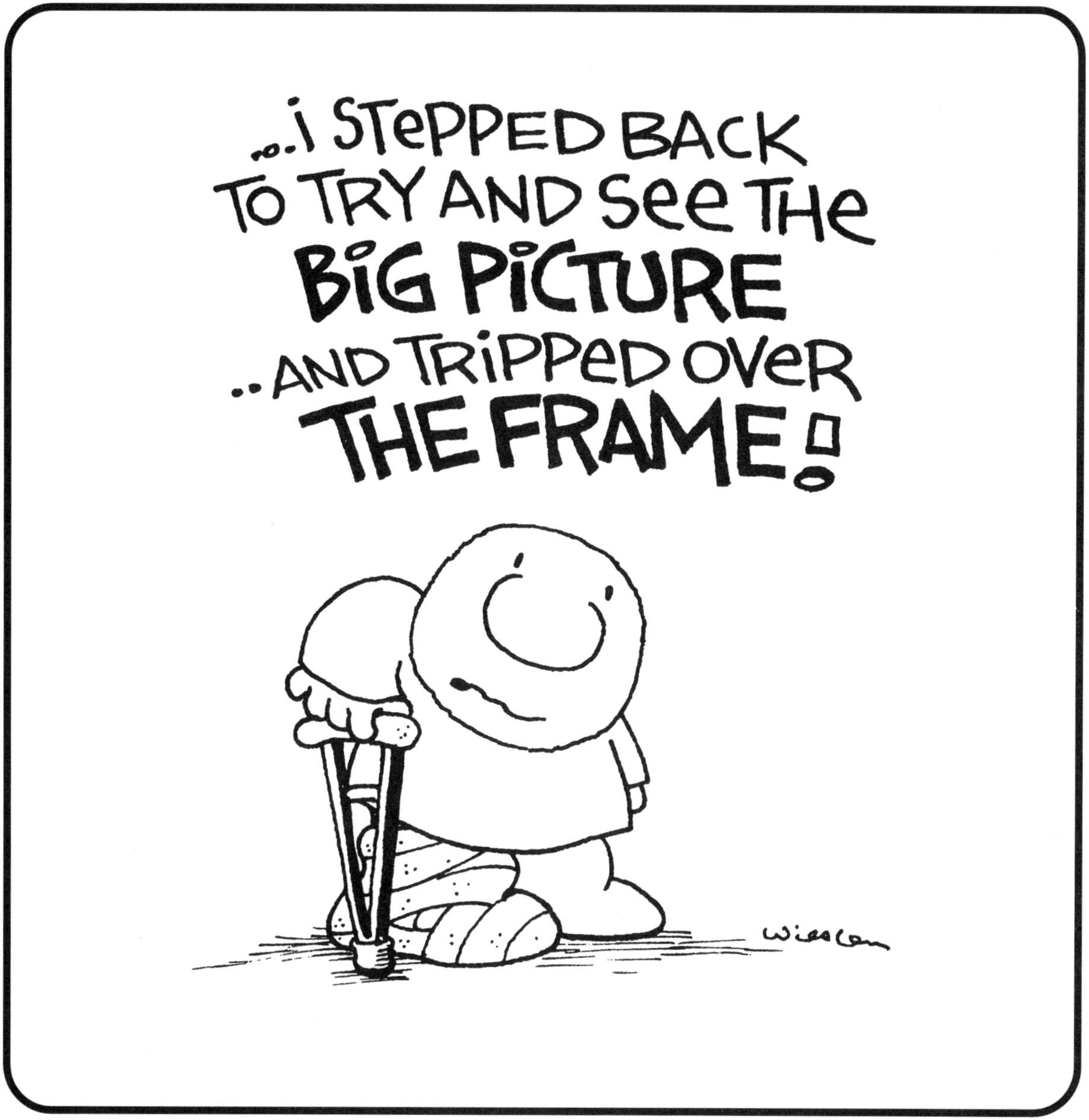
...i STEPPED BACK TO TRY AND SEE THE BIG PICTURE
..AND TRIPPED OVER THE FRAME!

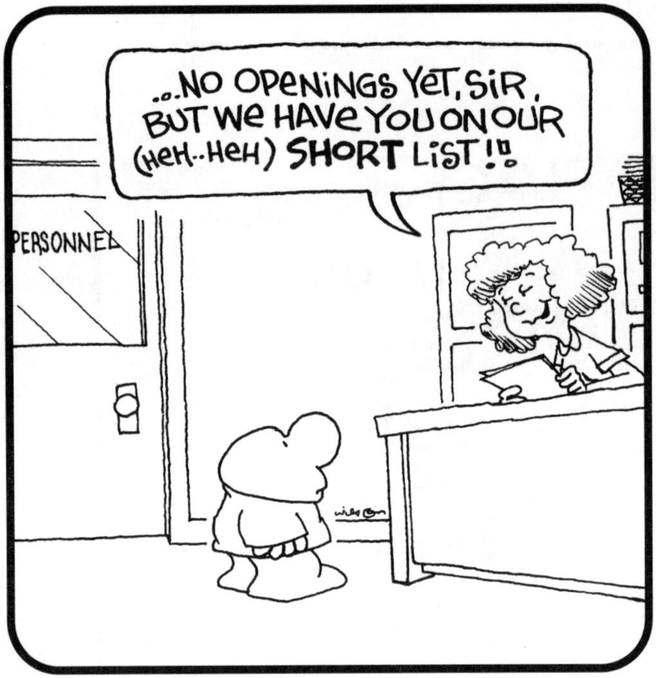
..NO OPENINGS YET, SIR, BUT WE HAVE YOU ON OUR (HEH..HEH) SHORT LIST !!
PERSONNEL

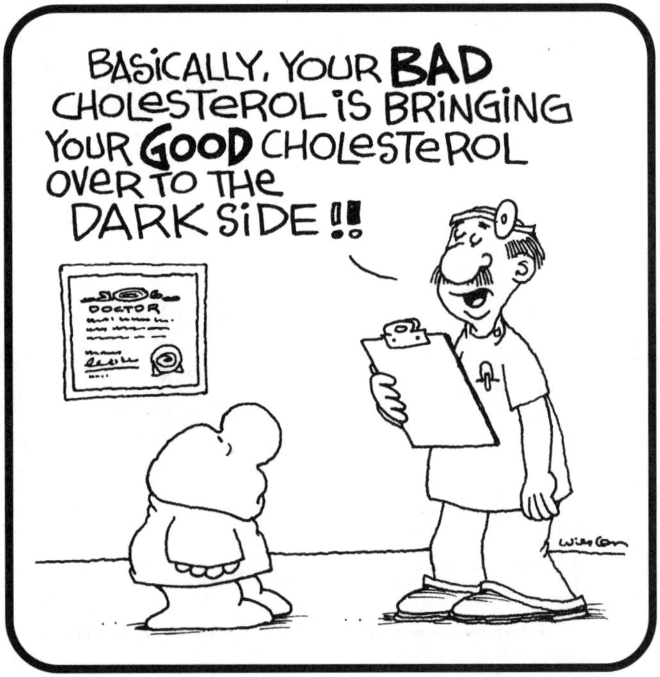
BASICALLY, YOUR BAD CHOLESTEROL IS BRINGING YOUR GOOD CHOLESTEROL OVER TO THE DARK SIDE !!
DOCTOR

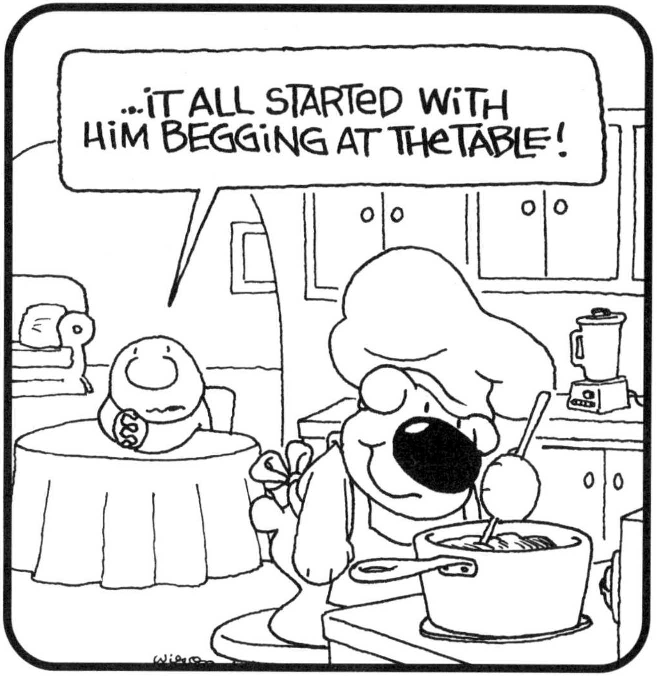
...IT ALL STARTED WITH HIM BEGGING AT THE TABLE!

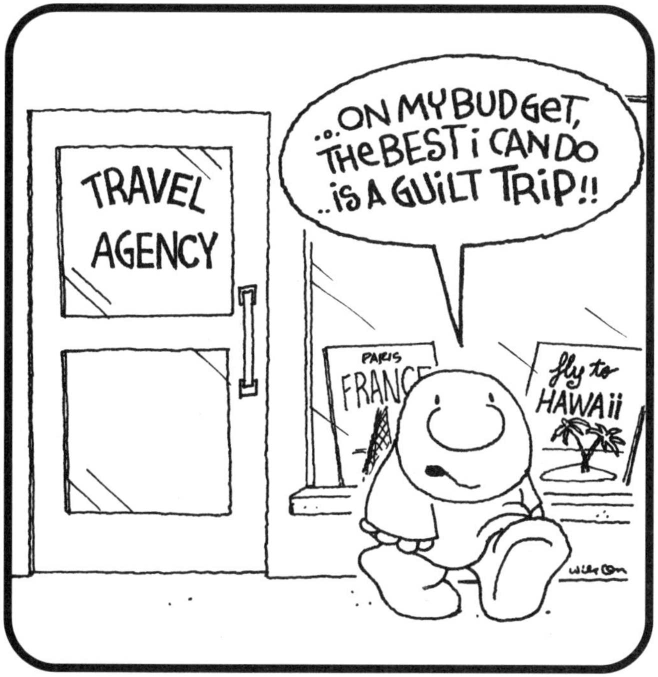
TRAVEL AGENCY
..ON MY BUDGET, THE BEST I CAN DO ..IS A GUILT TRIP!!
PARIS
FRANCE
fly to
HAWAii

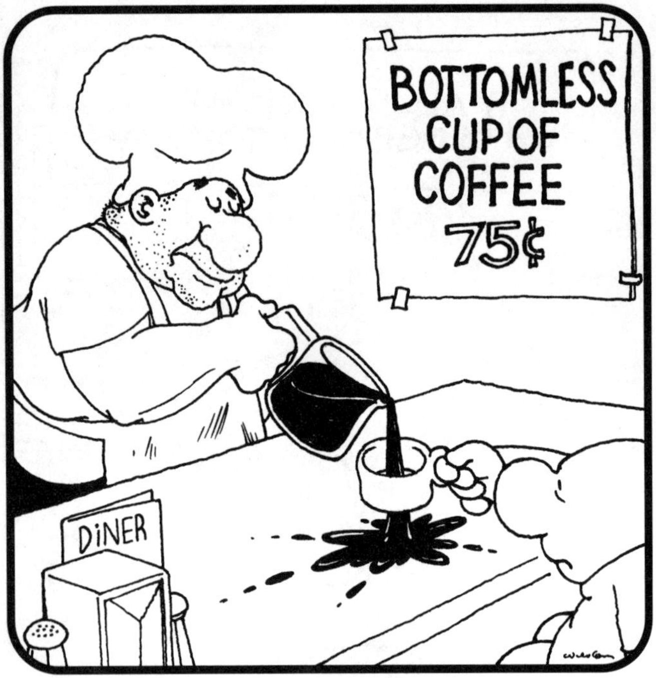
BOTTOMLESS
CUP OF
COFFEE
75¢
DiNER

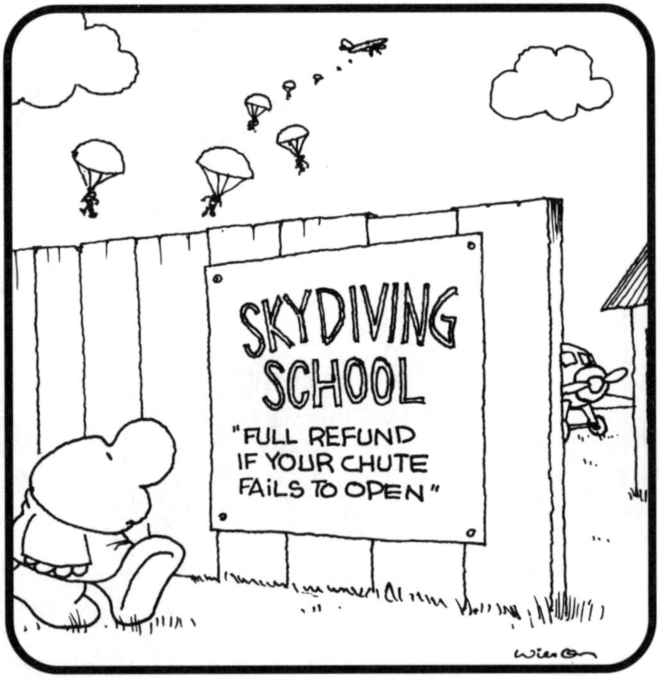
SKYDIVING
SCHOOL
"FULL REFUND
IF YOUR CHUTE
FAILS TO OPEN"

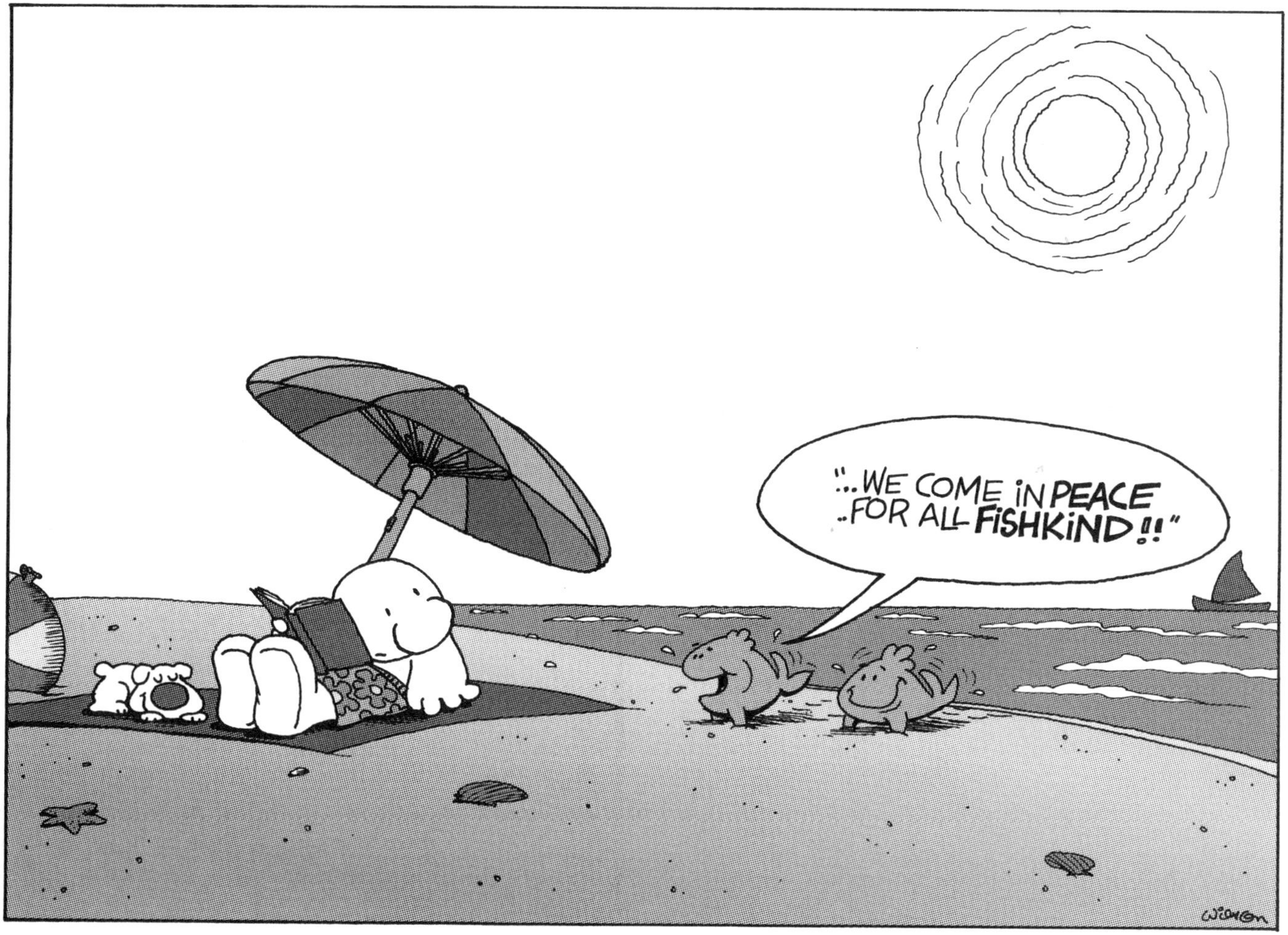
"..WE COME IN PEACE ..FOR ALL FISHKIND!!"

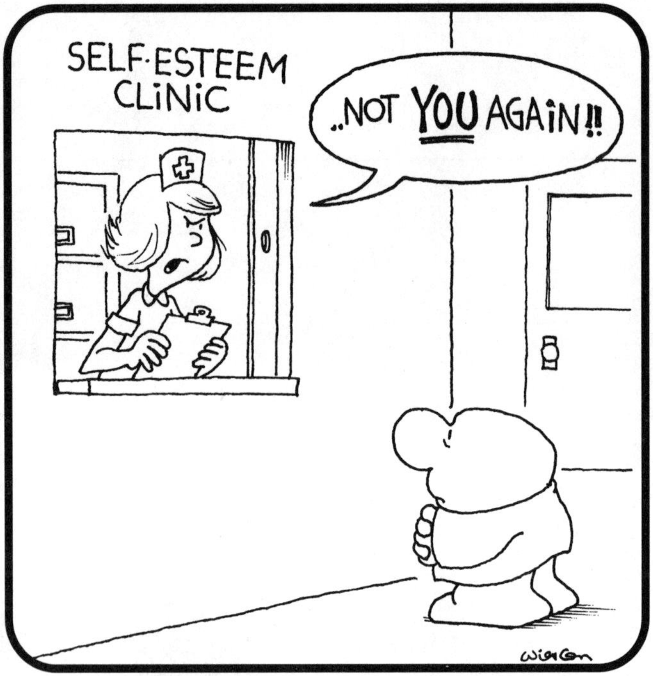
SELF-ESTEEM CLINIC
..NOT YOU AGAIN!!
wilson

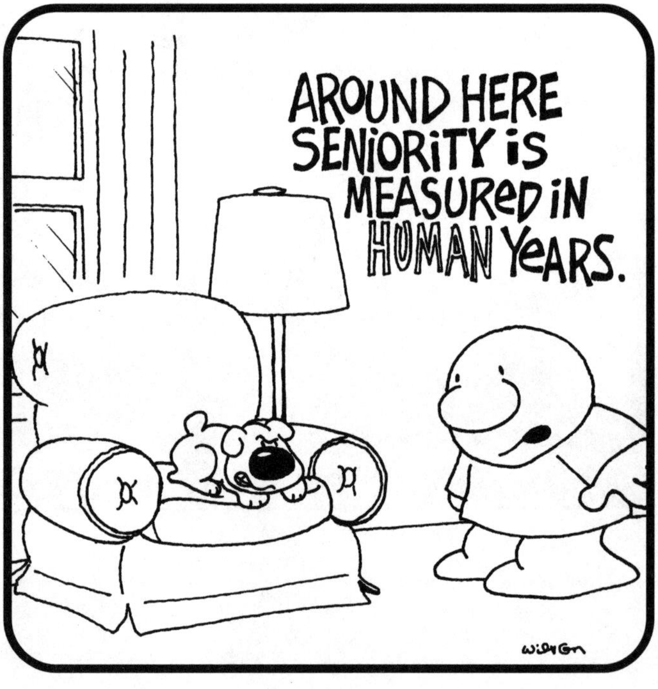
AROUND HERE SENIORITY is MEASURED IN HUMAN YEARS.
wilson

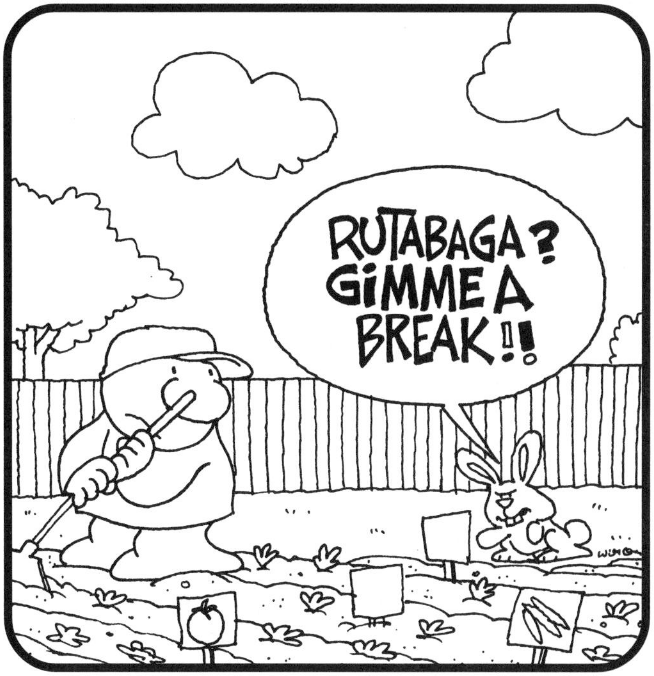
RUTABAGA? GIMME A BREAK!!

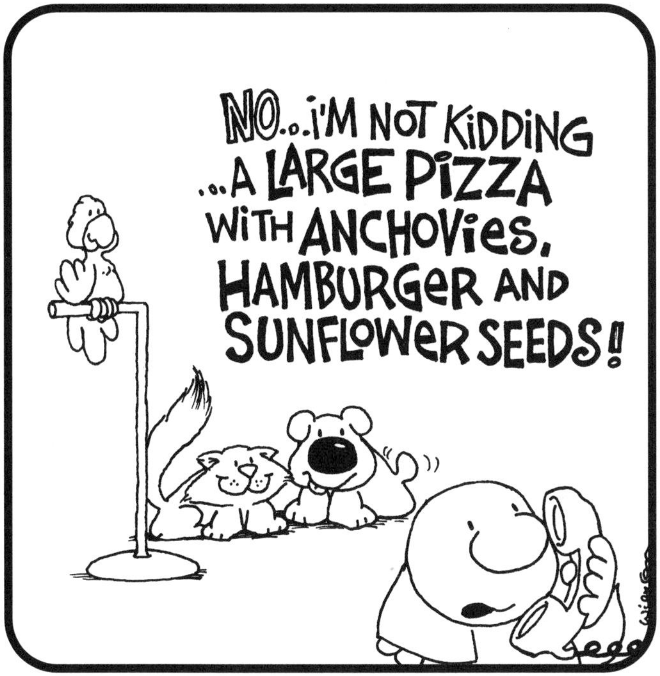
NO...I'M NOT KIDDING ...A LARGE PIZZA WITH ANCHOVIES, HAMBURGER AND SUNFLOWER SEEDS!

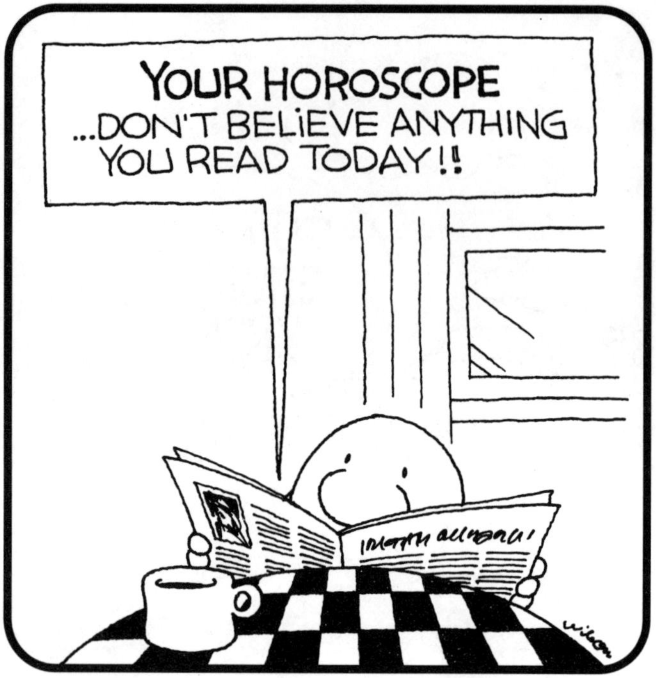
YOUR HOROSCOPE
...DON'T BELIEVE ANYTHING
YOU READ TODAY!!

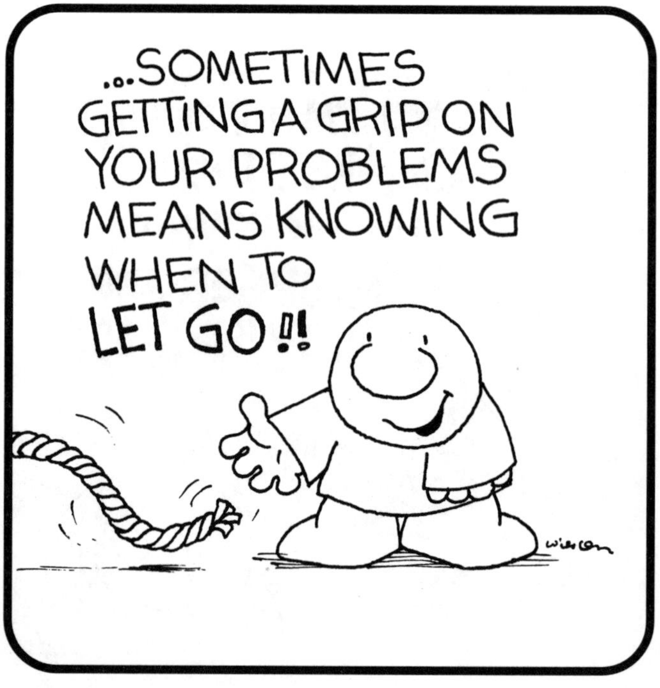
...SOMETIMES
GETTING A GRIP ON
YOUR PROBLEMS
MEANS KNOWING
WHEN TO
LET GO!!

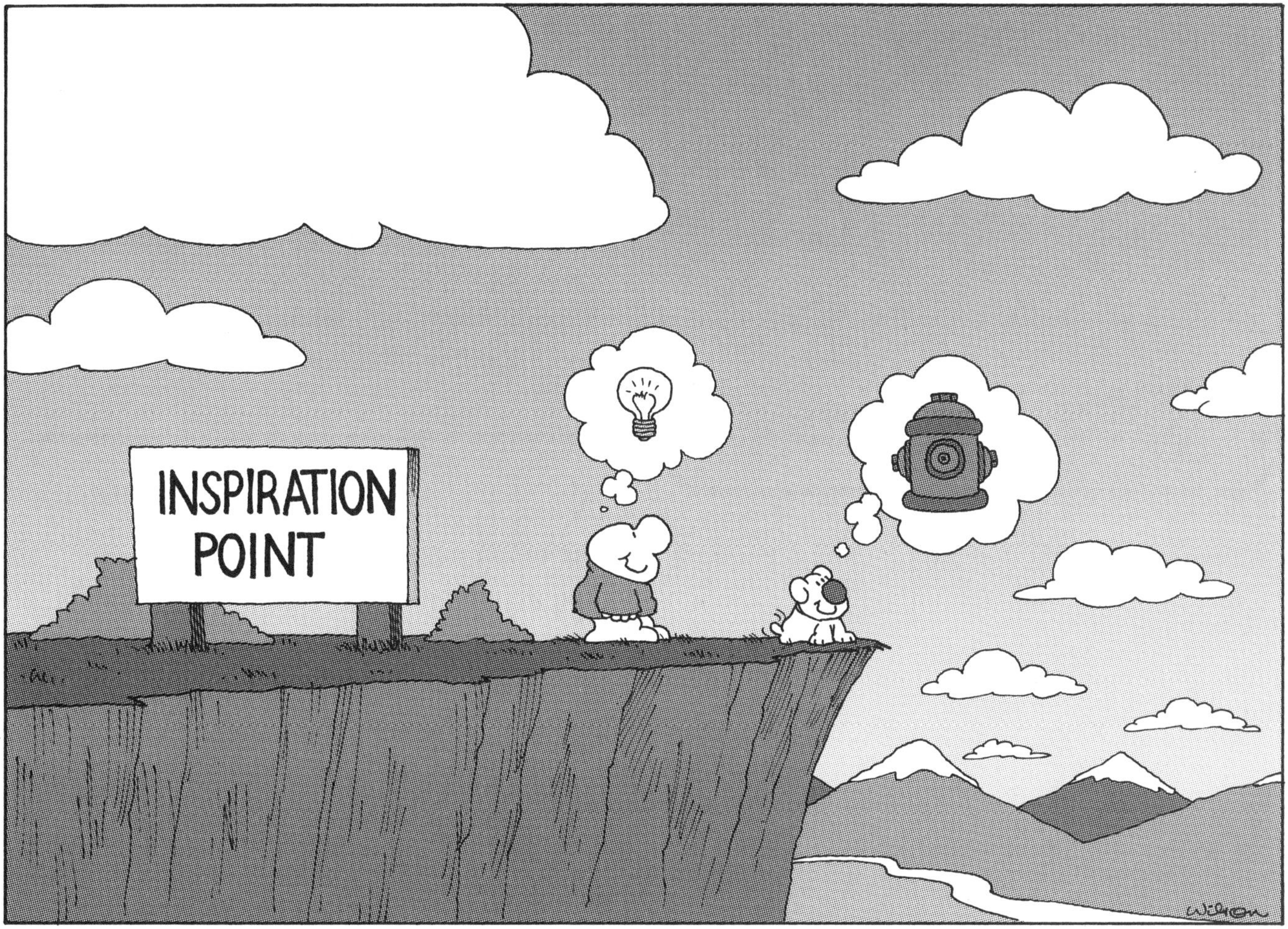
INSPIRATION POINT

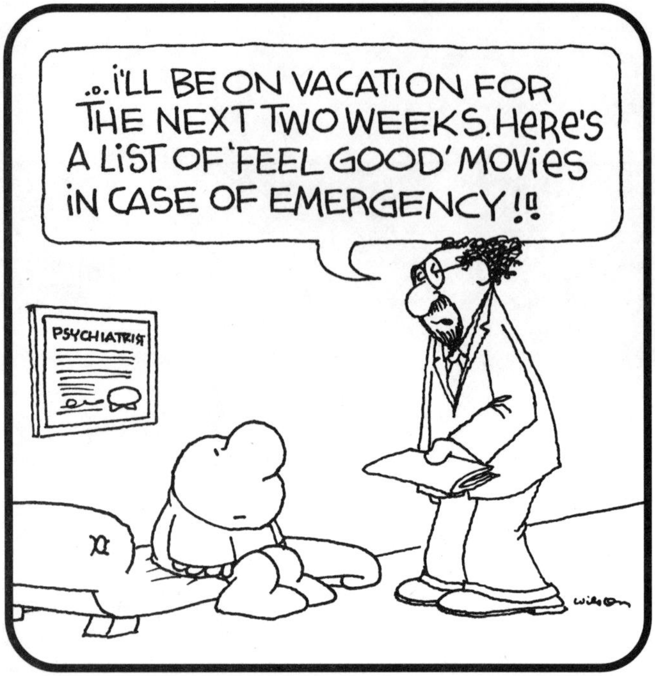
..I'LL BE ON VACATION FOR THE NEXT TWO WEEKS. HERE'S A LIST OF 'FEEL GOOD' MOVIES IN CASE OF EMERGENCY!!
PSYCHIATRIST
wilson

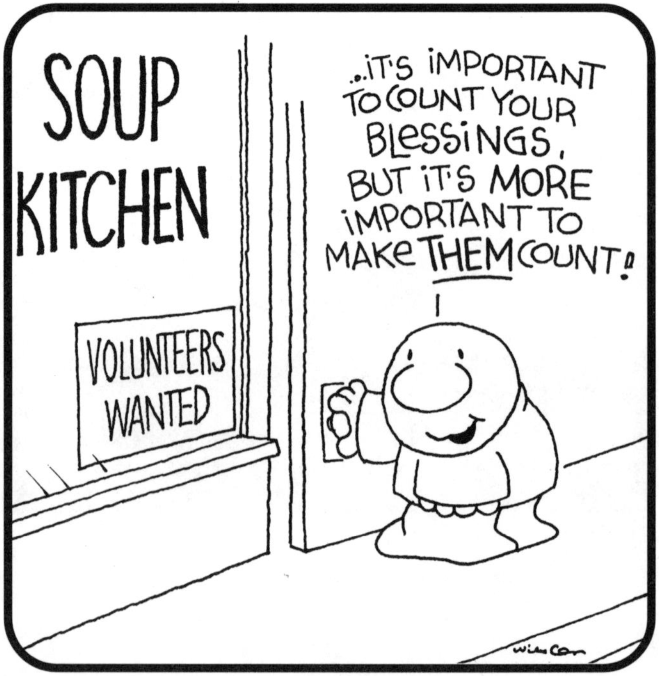
SOUP KITCHEN
VOLUNTEERS WANTED
..IT'S IMPORTANT TO COUNT YOUR BLESSINGS, BUT IT'S MORE IMPORTANT TO MAKE THEM COUNT!
wilson

..YOU KNOW, IGGY, WHEN I WAS A YOUNGSTER, EVERYTHING EXCITED ME AND NOTHING SLOWED ME DOWN!!
.. EVEN AS A TEENAGER, I WAS ALWAYS UP FOR A LI'L MISCHIEF IF THE CONDITIONS WERE RIGHT!!
..I SETTLED DOWN SOME AS A YOUNG MAN, BUT I WAS STILL QUICK TO RILE.
..NOW, I'M OLD AND I CAN'T REMEMBER THE LAST TIME I GOT WORKED UP ABOUT ANYTHING!!
..I GUESS THERE'S A LESSON IN THERE SOMEWHERE, MR. PENDLETON.
YEP!
WHAT GROWS UP...
.. MUST CALM DOWN!

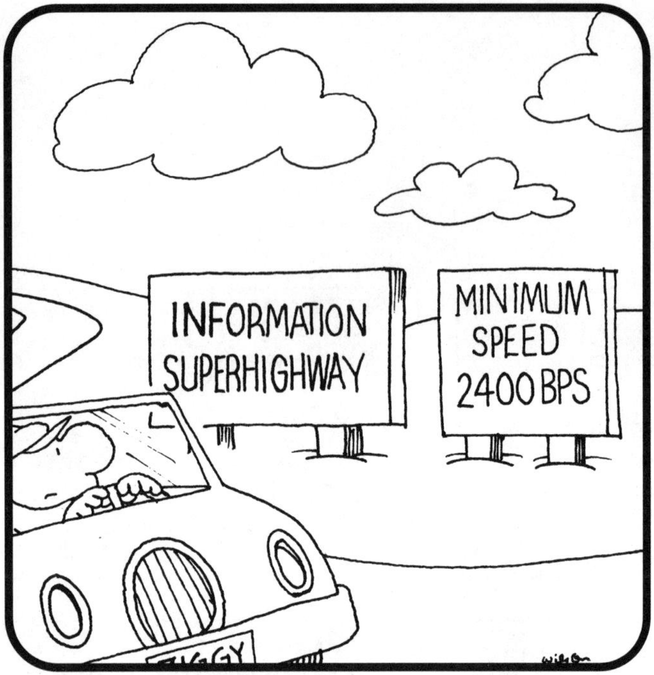
INFORMATION SUPERHIGHWAY
MINIMUM SPEED 2400 BPS

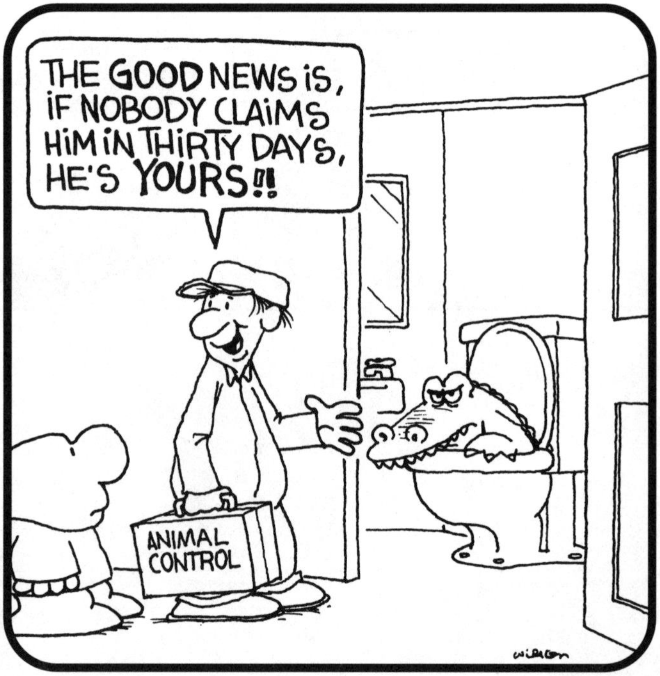
THE GOOD NEWS IS, IF NOBODY CLAIMS HIM IN THIRTY DAYS, HE'S YOURS!!
ANIMAL CONTROL

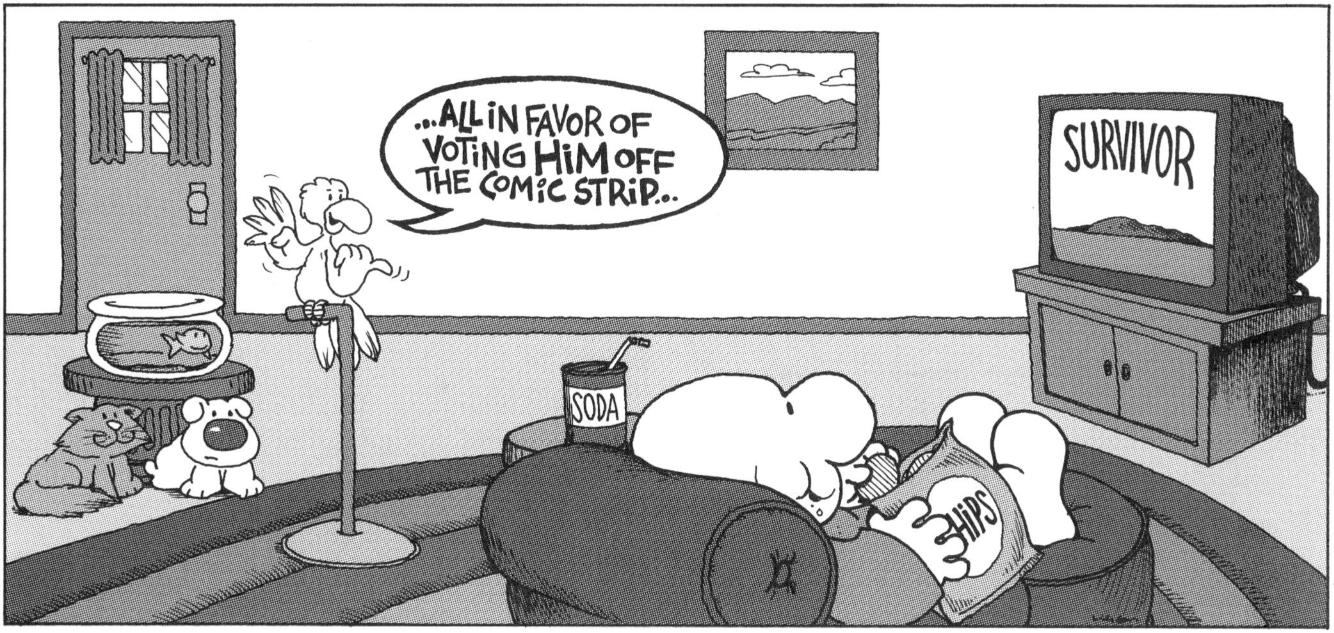
...ALL IN FAVOR OF VOTING HIM OFF THE COMIC STRIP...
SURVIVOR
SODA
CHIPS

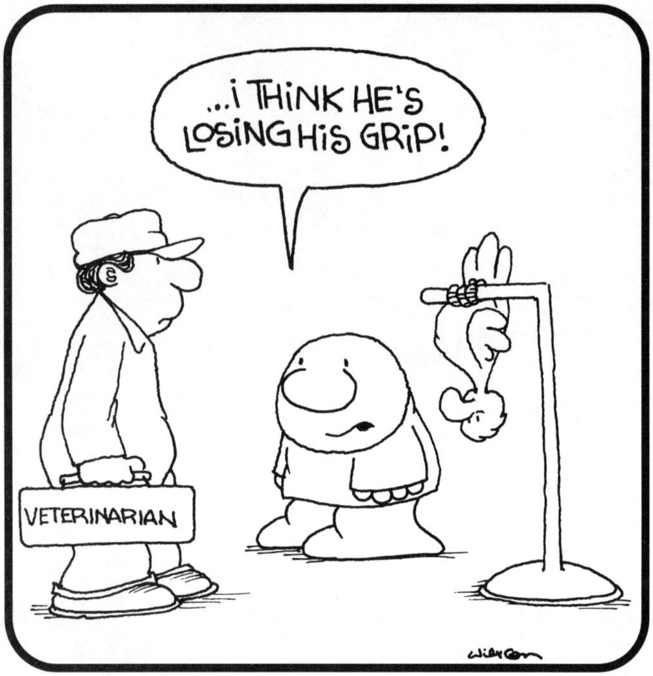
...i THiNK HE'S LOSiNG HiS GRiP!
VETERINARIAN

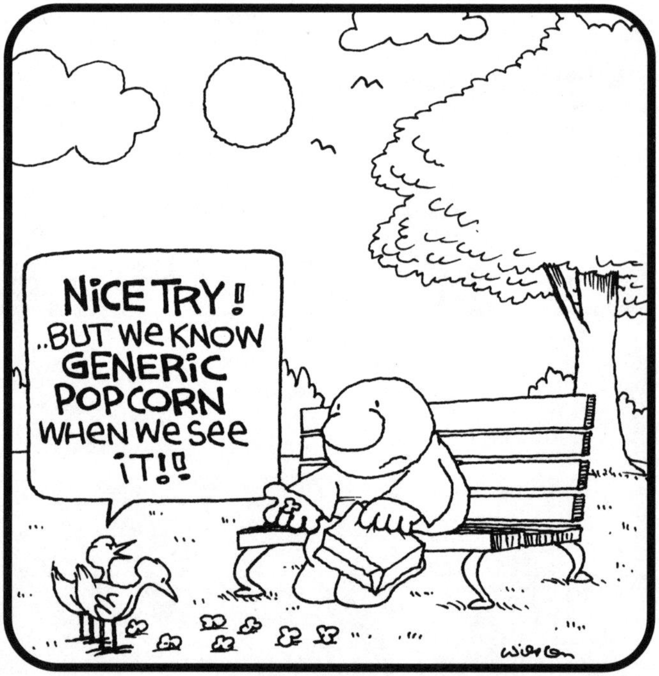
NiCE TRY! ..BUT WE KNOW GENERiC POPCORN WHEN WE SEE iT!!

COMPLAINTS
...I HAVE A COMPLAINT ABOUT THIS HAIR RESTORER I BOUGHT!
COMPLAINTS
HAIR RESTORER
YEAH? WHAT IS IT?
COMPLAINTS
HAIR RESTORER
...LOOK, MAC... THE BOX SAYS HAIR RESTORER! ..RIGHT?
COMPLAINTS
HAIR RESTORER
RIGHT!
..IT DOESN'T SAY HAIRS RESTORER, DOES IT?
HAIR RESTORER
COMPLAINTS
CLOSED
NO

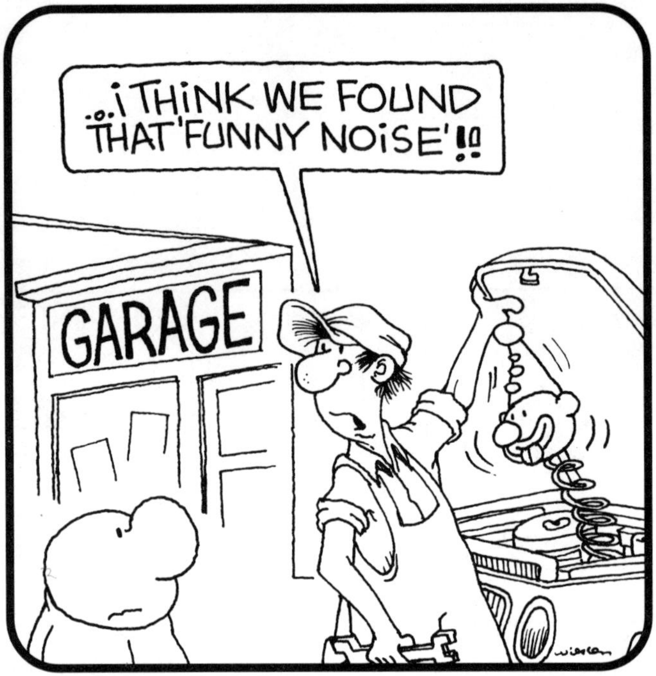
..i THINK WE FOUND THAT 'FUNNY NOISE'!!
GARAGE

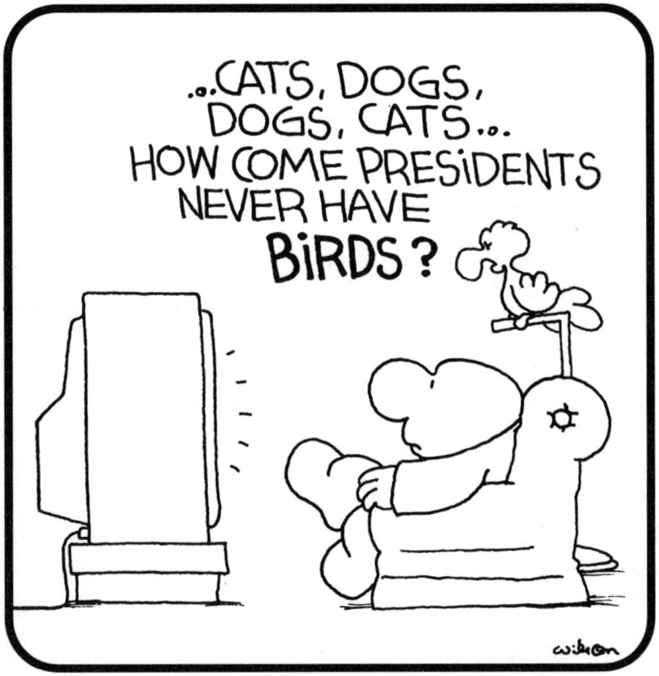
..CATS, DOGS, DOGS, CATS... HOW COME PRESIDENTS NEVER HAVE BIRDS?

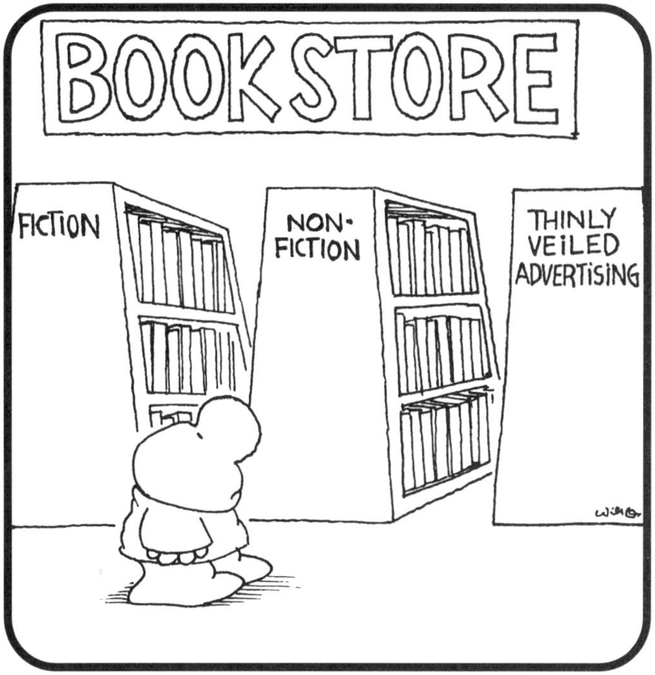
BOOKSTORE
FICTION
NON-FICTION
THINLY VEILED ADVERTISING

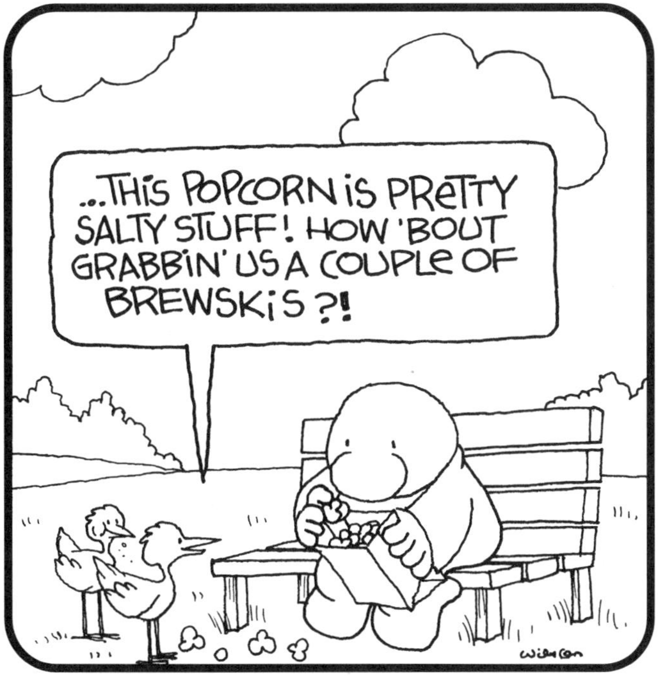
...THIS POPCORN IS PRETTY SALTY STUFF! HOW 'BOUT GRABBIN' US A COUPLE OF BREWSKIS ?!

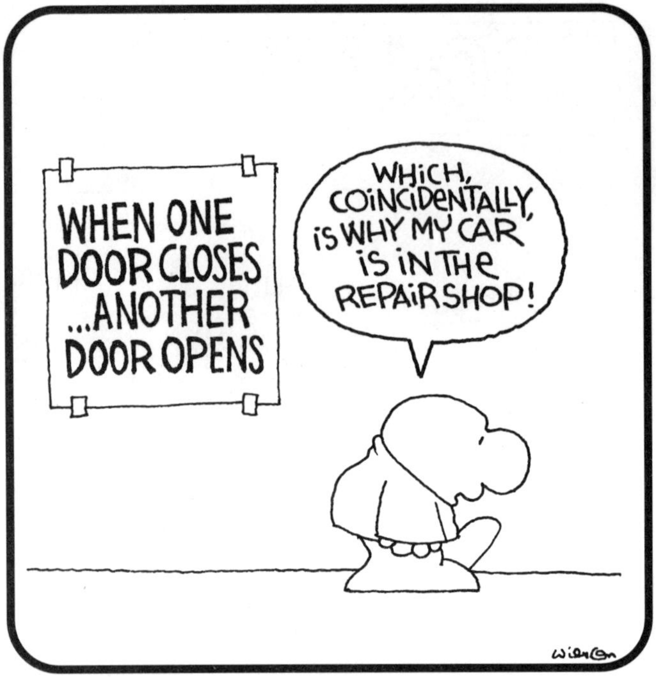
WHEN ONE DOOR CLOSES ...ANOTHER DOOR OPENS
WHICH, COINCIDENTALLY, IS WHY MY CAR IS IN THE REPAIRSHOP!

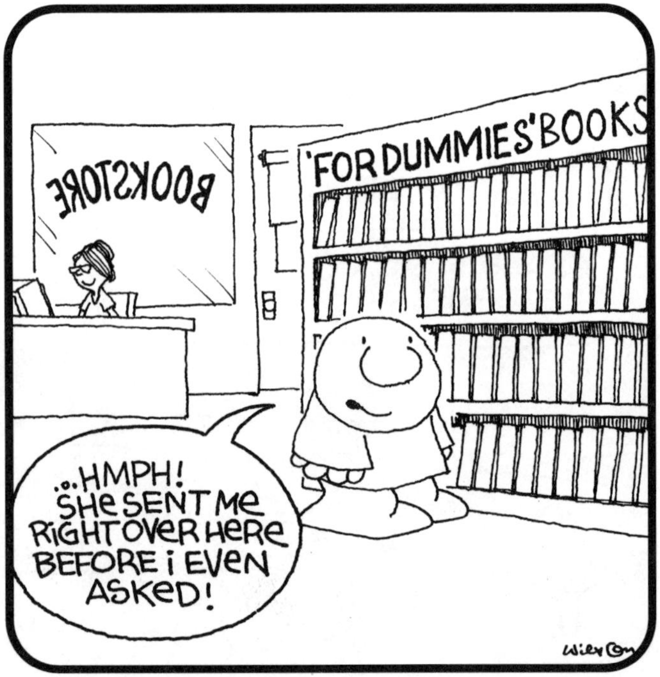
BOOKSTORE
'FOR DUMMIES' BOOKS
..HMPH! SHE SENT ME RIGHT OVER HERE BEFORE I EVEN ASKED!

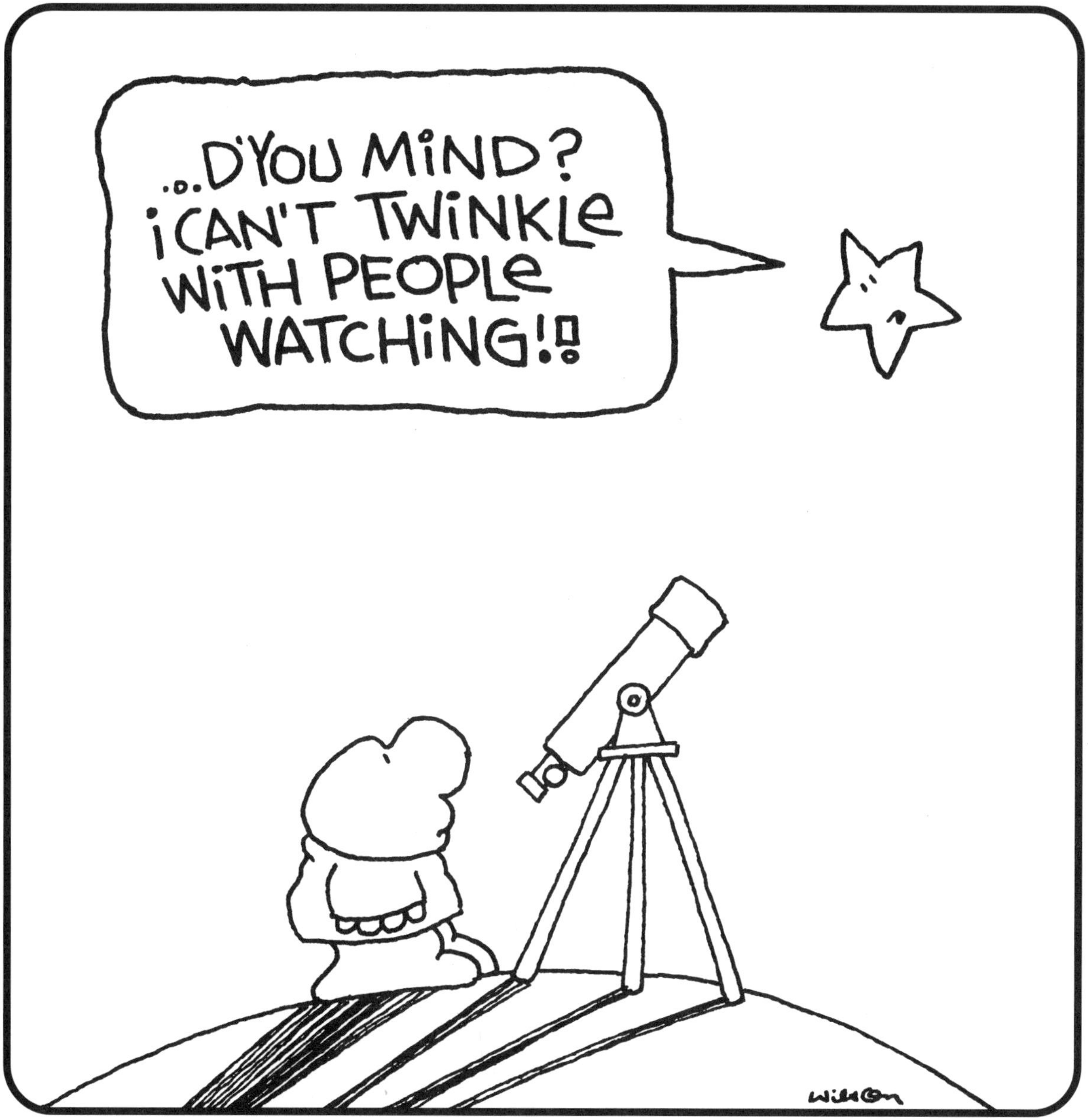
..D'YOU MIND? I CAN'T TWINKLE WITH PEOPLE WATCHING!!

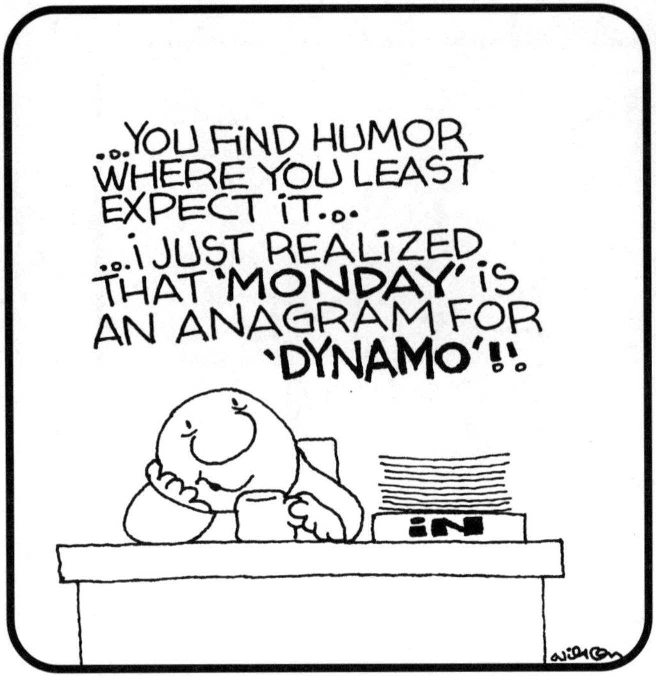
..YOU FIND HUMOR WHERE YOU LEAST EXPECT IT...
...I JUST REALIZED THAT 'MONDAY' IS AN ANAGRAM FOR 'DYNAMO'!!
IN
wilson

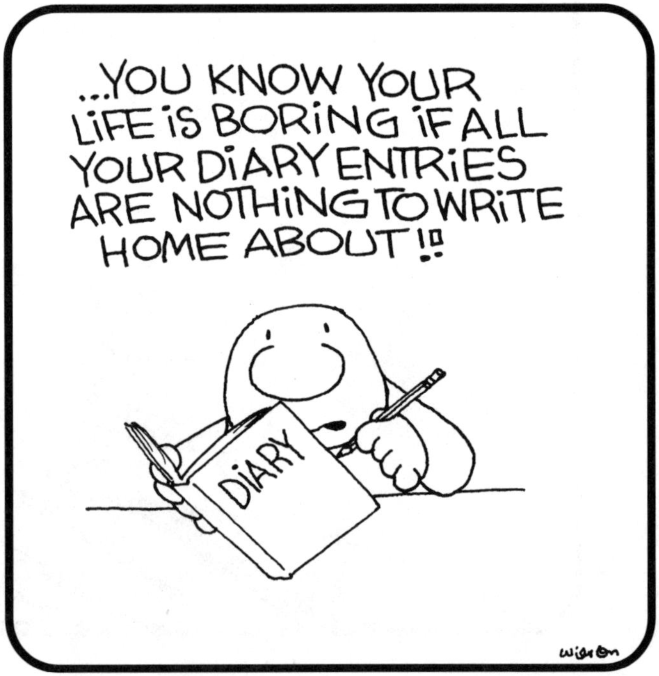
...YOU KNOW YOUR LIFE IS BORING IF ALL YOUR DIARY ENTRIES ARE NOTHING TO WRITE HOME ABOUT!!
DIARY
wilson

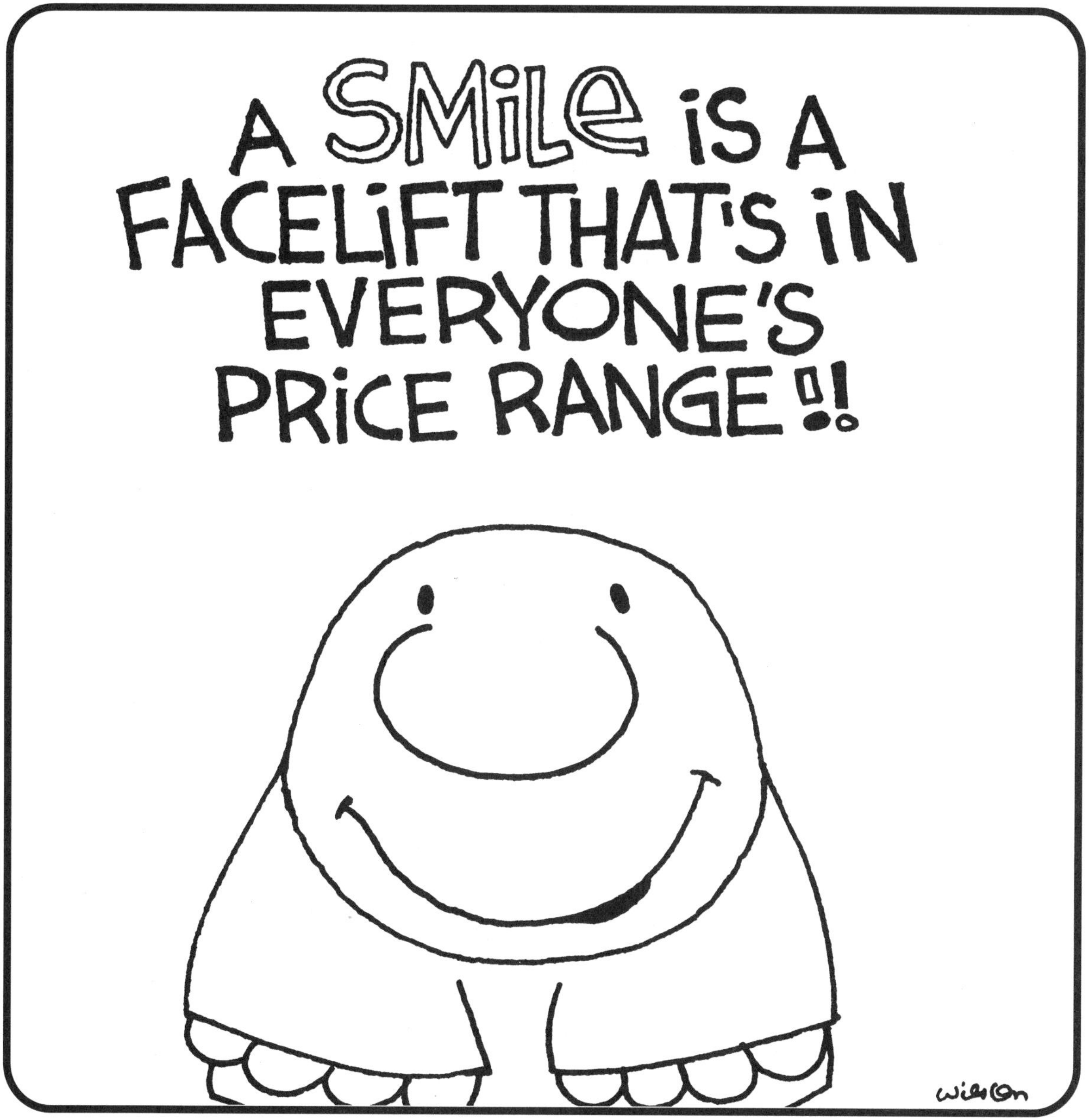
A SMILE IS A FACELIFT THAT'S IN EVERYONE'S PRICE RANGE!!
wilson

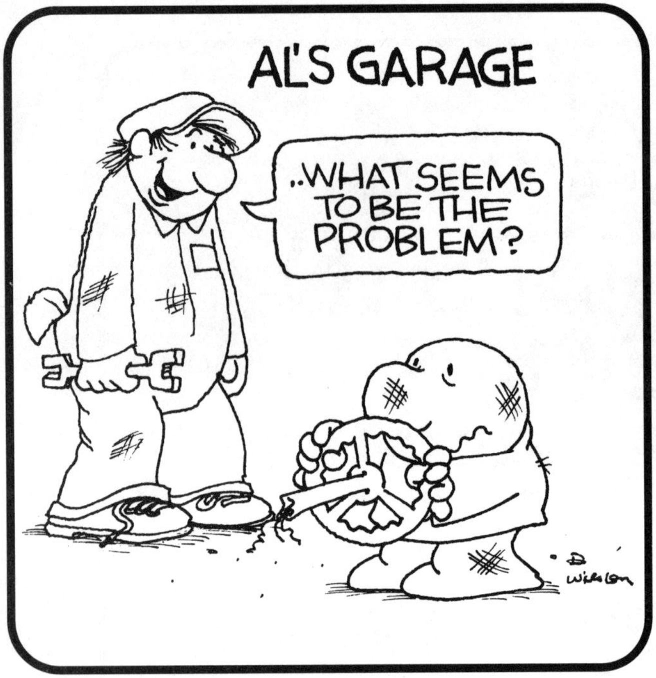
AL'S GARAGE
..WHAT SEEMS TO BE THE PROBLEM?

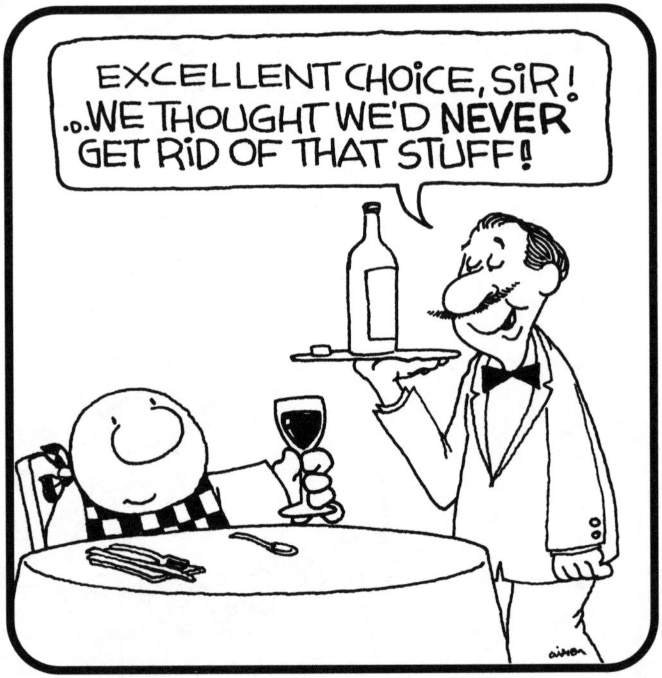
EXCELLENT CHOICE, SIR! ..WE THOUGHT WE'D **NEVER** GET RID OF THAT STUFF!

LOOKIN' IN THE MIRROR IS ALWAYS A BIT OF A SURPRISE.

NO MATTER HOW OLD I GET, MY MENTAL IMAGE IS ALWAYS OF MYSELF AS A YOUNG MAN!

INSTEAD, WHAT I SEE IS AN ADULT LOOKING BACK AT ME WITH A PUZZLED EXPRESSION!

..I REALLY HOPE IT'S A SIGN OF BEING YOUNG AT HEART!

..'CAUSE I'D SURE HATE TO THINK THAT I'M JUST BEING SLOW ON THE UPTAKE!!

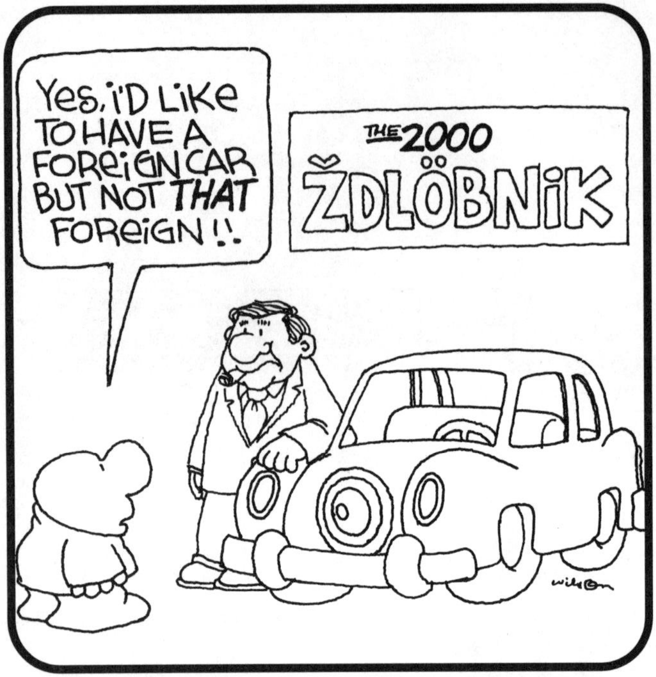
YES, I'D LIKE TO HAVE A FOREIGN CAR BUT NOT *THAT* FOREIGN!!
THE 2000
ŽDLÖBNIK

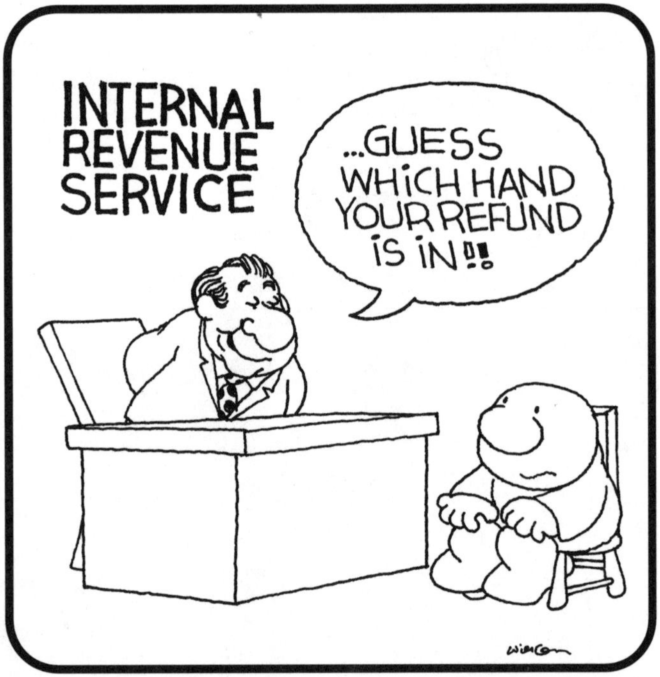
INTERNAL REVENUE SERVICE
...GUESS WHICH HAND YOUR REFUND IS IN!!

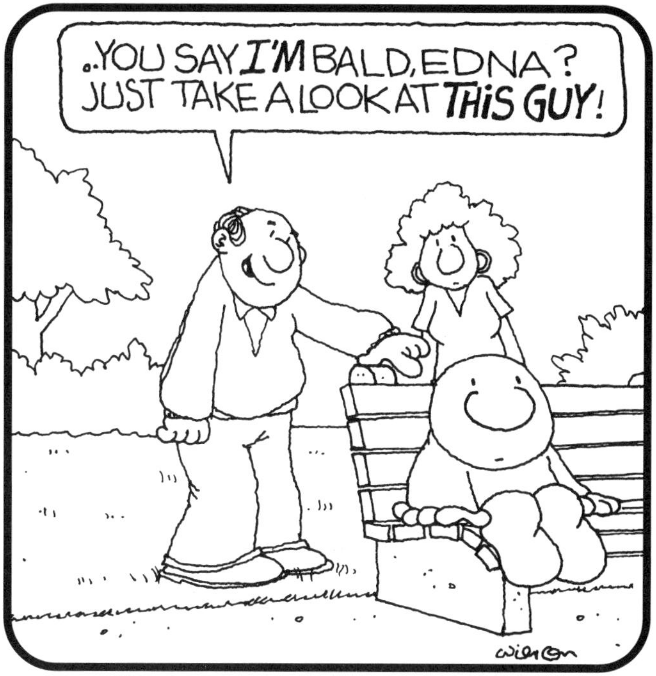
..YOU SAY I'M BALD, EDNA? JUST TAKE A LOOK AT THIS GUY!
wilson

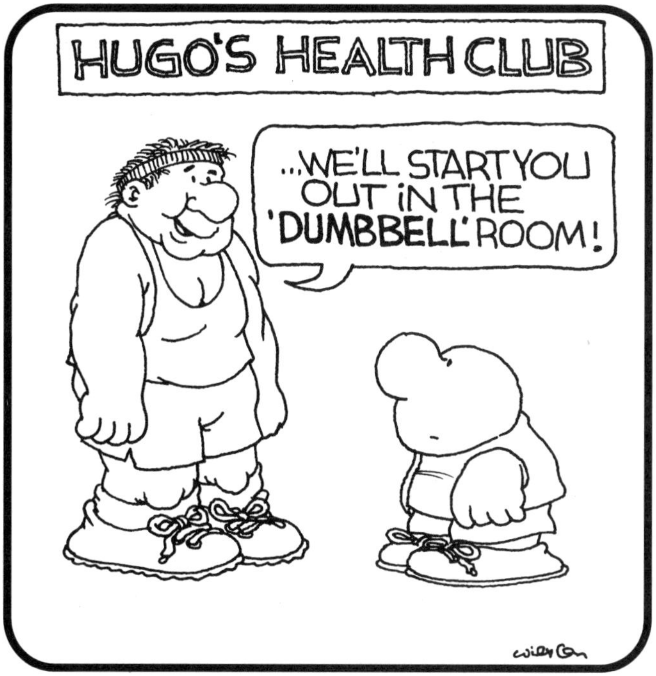
HUGO'S HEALTH CLUB
...WE'LL START YOU OUT IN THE 'DUMBBELL' ROOM!
wilson

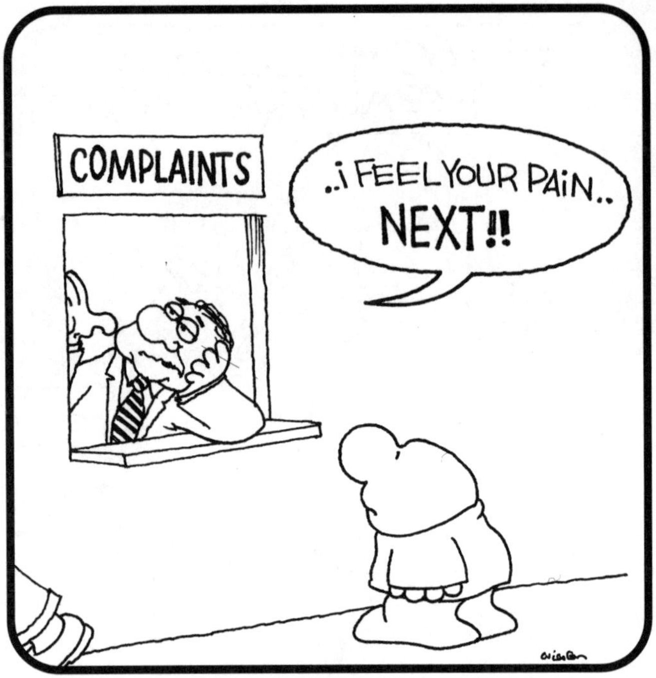
COMPLAINTS
..i FEEL YOUR PAIN.. NEXT!!

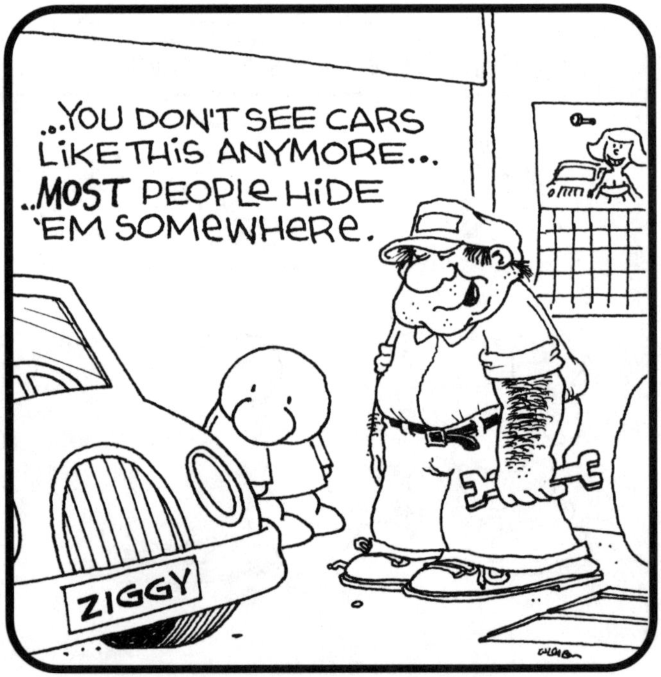
..YOU DON'T SEE CARS LIKE THIS ANYMORE... ..MOST PEOPLE HIDE 'EM SOMEWHERE.
ZIGGY

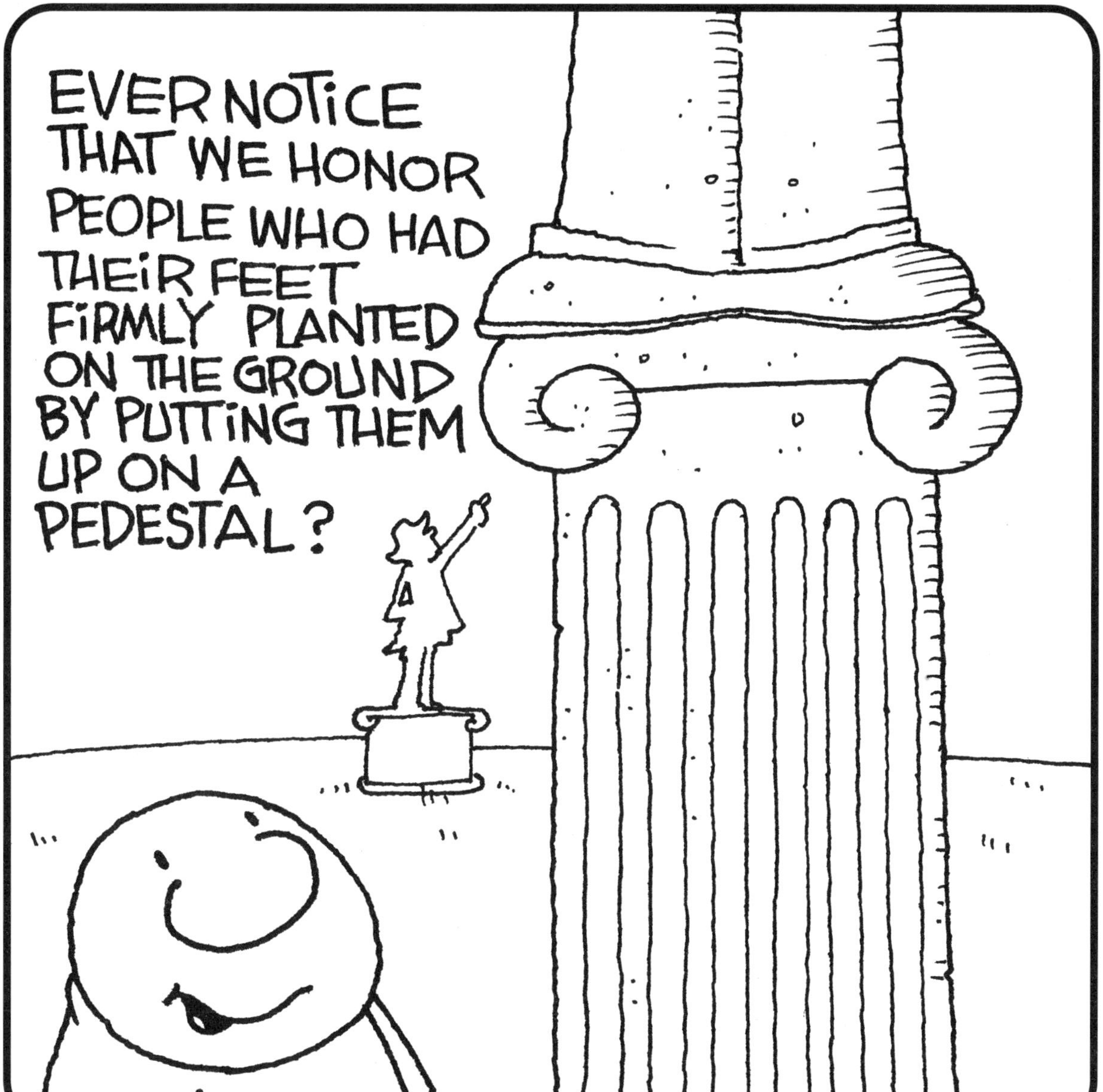
EVER NOTICE THAT WE HONOR PEOPLE WHO HAD THEIR FEET FIRMLY PLANTED ON THE GROUND BY PUTTING THEM UP ON A PEDESTAL?

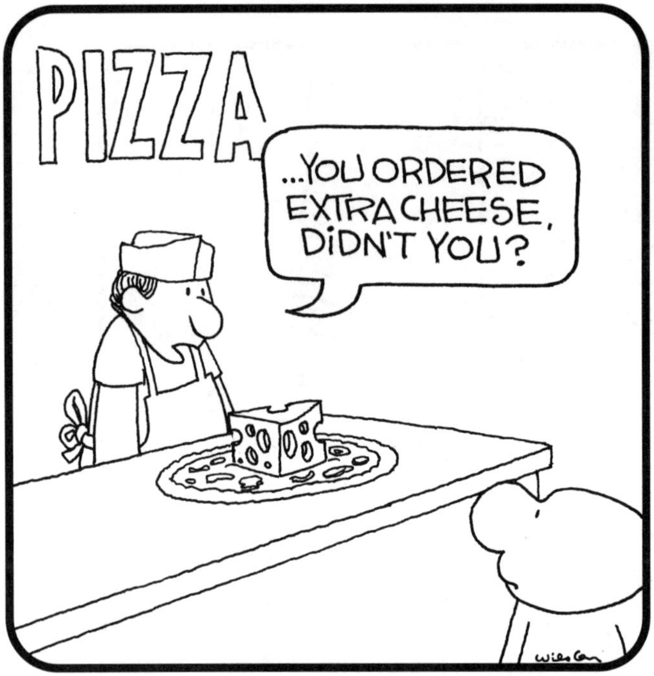
PIZZA
...YOU ORDERED EXTRA CHEESE, DIDN'T YOU?
Wiley

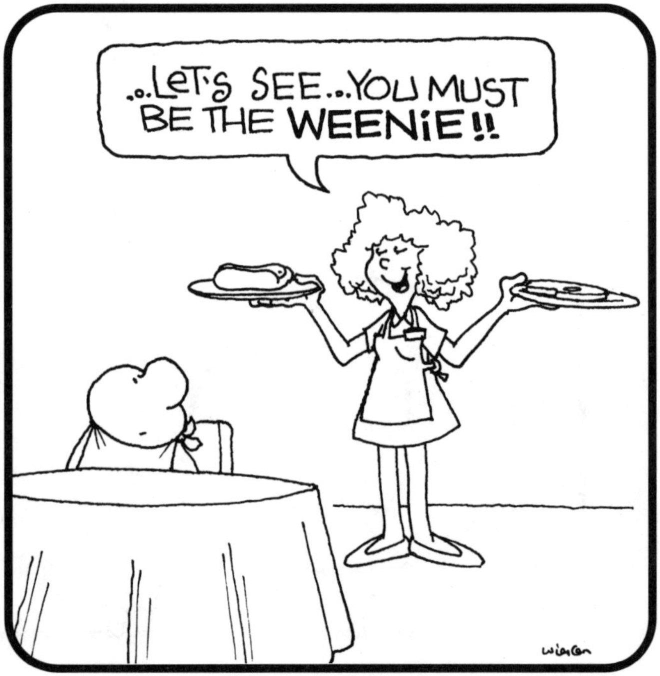
...LET'S SEE...YOU MUST BE THE **WEENIE**!!
Wiley

LADDER OF SUCCESS
ZIGGY— KNOCKED ONCE! SORRY YOU WERE OUT! -opportunity
CASH MACHINE
CHECKING ACCOUNT...ER WHAT CHECKING ACCOUNT?
1
...SOME DAYS, I FEEL LIKE MY LIFE IS A 'WIN-WHEN?' SITUATION!!

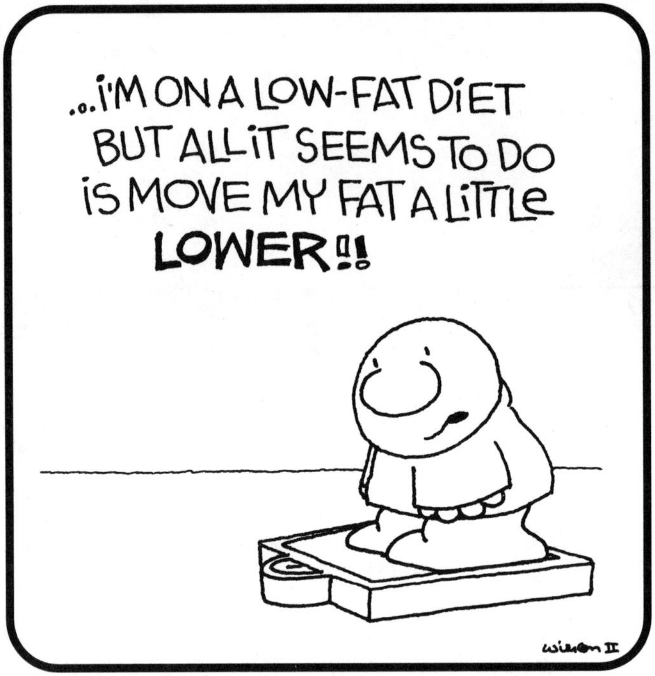
...I'M ON A LOW-FAT DIET BUT ALL IT SEEMS TO DO IS MOVE MY FAT A LITTLE LOWER!!

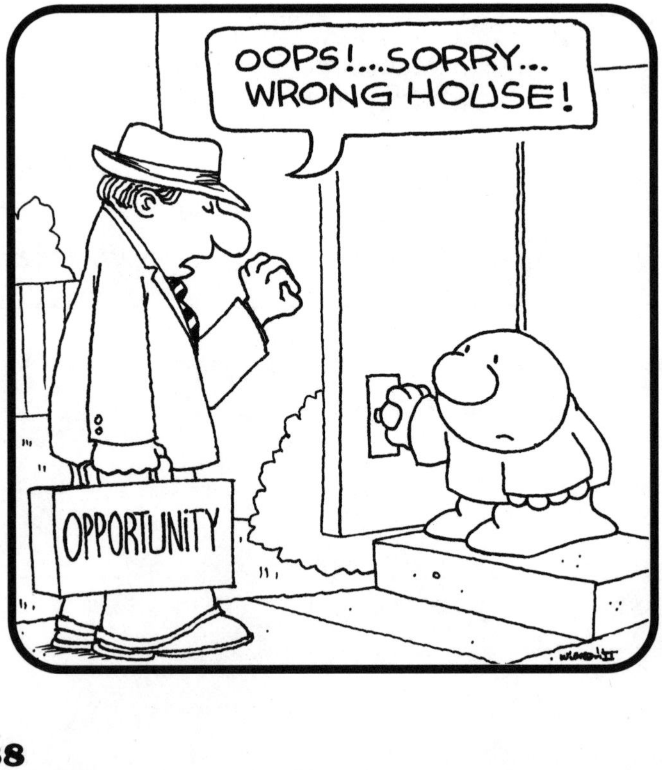
OOPS!...SORRY... WRONG HOUSE!
OPPORTUNITY

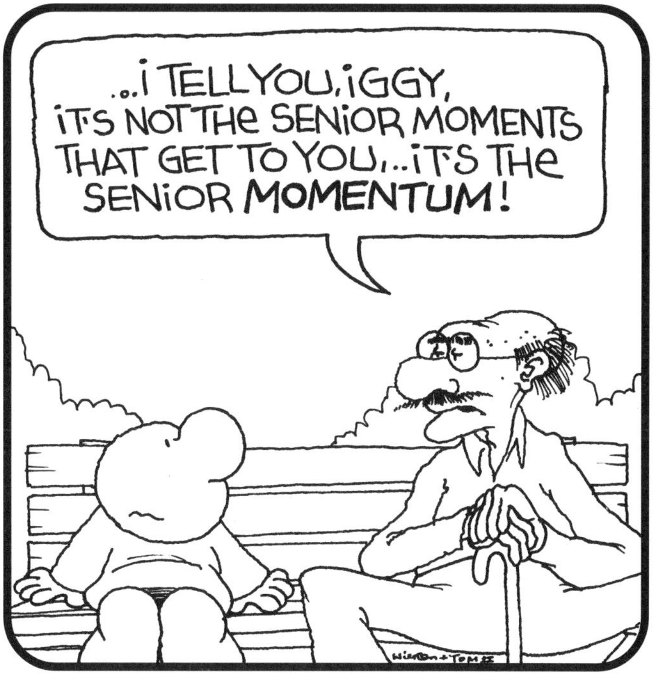
...i TELL YOU, iGGY, iT'S NOT THE SENiOR MOMENTS THAT GET TO YOU,...iT'S THE SENiOR **MOMENTUM**!

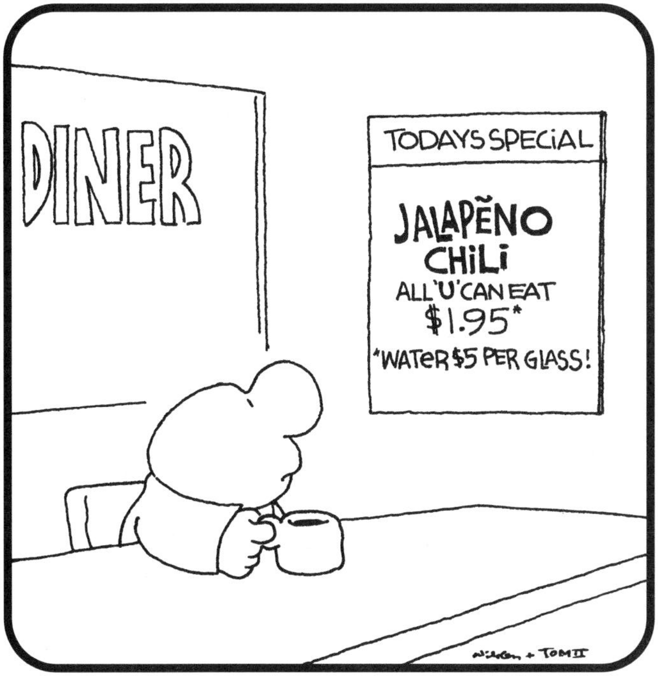
DINER
TODAYS SPECiAL
JALAPEÑO CHiLi
ALL 'U' CAN EAT
$1.95*
*WATER $5 PER GLASS!

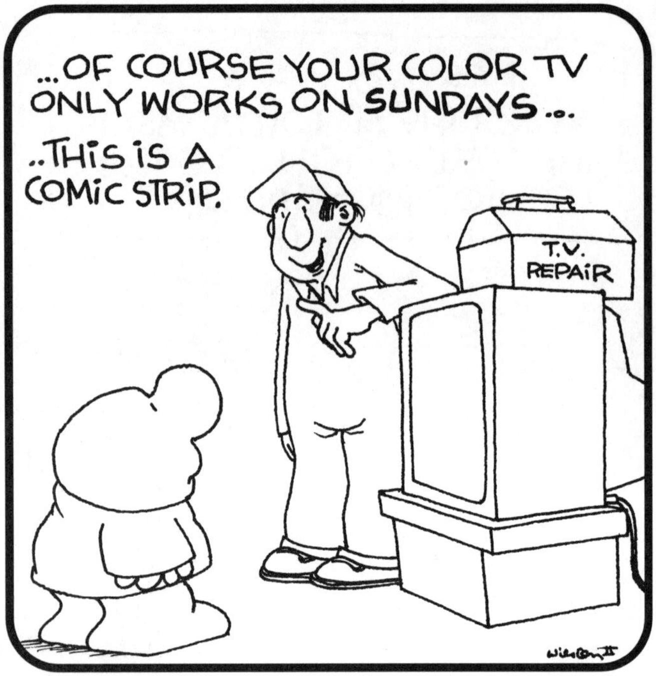
...OF COURSE YOUR COLOR TV ONLY WORKS ON SUNDAYS...
..THIS IS A COMIC STRIP.
T.V. REPAIR

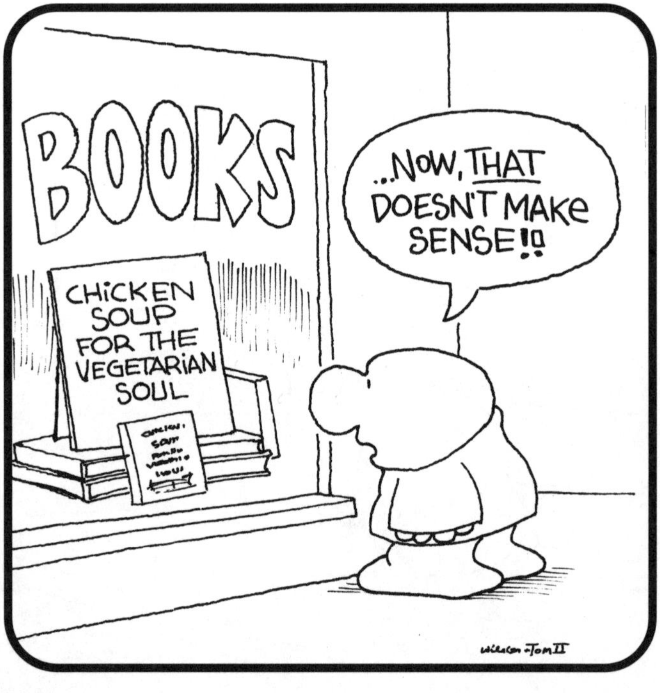
BOOKS
CHICKEN SOUP FOR THE VEGETARIAN SOUL
...NOW, THAT DOESN'T MAKE SENSE!!

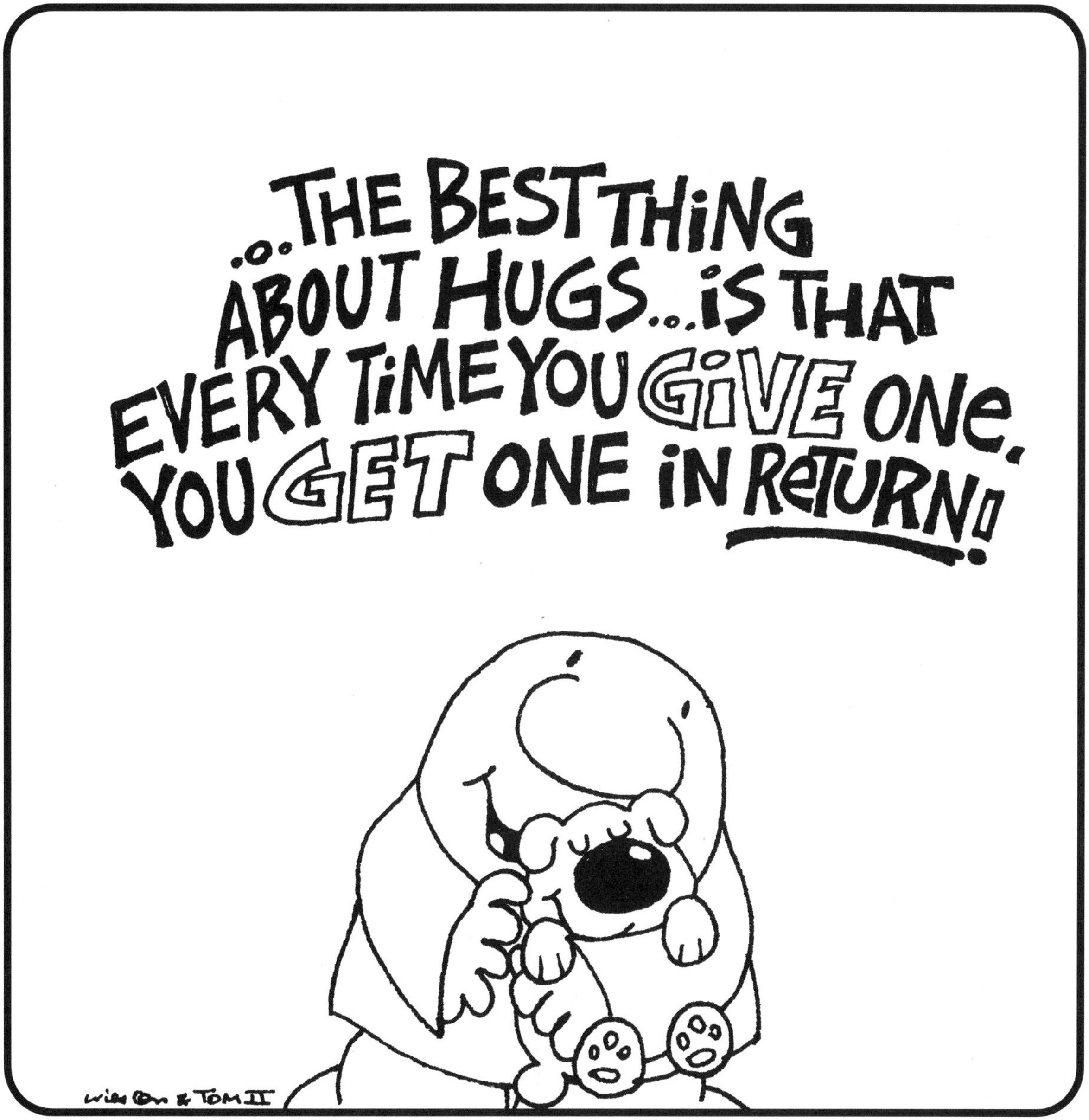
...THE BEST THING ABOUT HUGS...IS THAT EVERY TIME YOU GIVE ONE, YOU GET ONE IN RETURN!

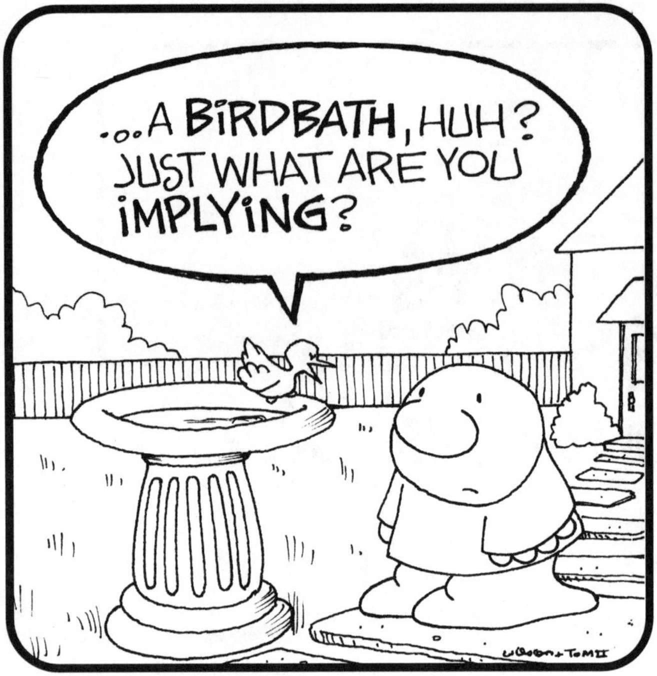
...A BIRDBATH, HUH? JUST WHAT ARE YOU IMPLYING?

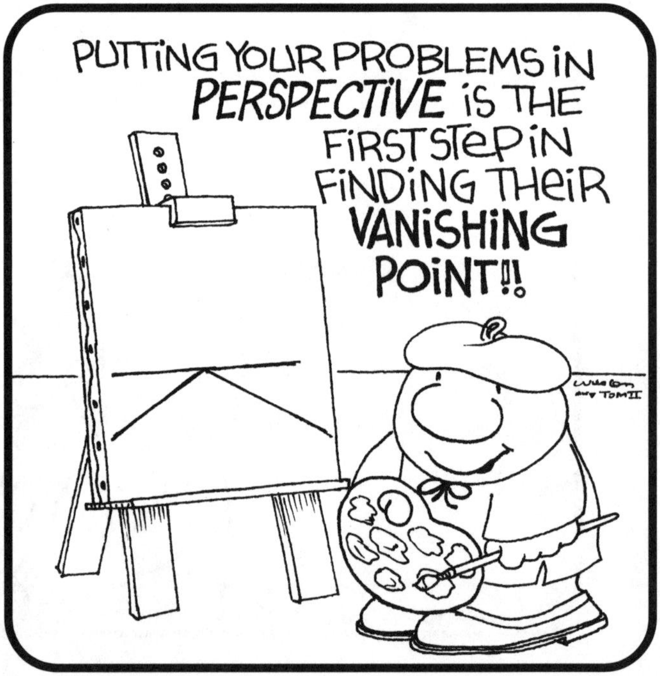
PUTTING YOUR PROBLEMS IN PERSPECTIVE IS THE FIRST STEP IN FINDING THEIR VANISHING POINT!!

..i'M HERE FOR MY CHECK-UP!
DOCTOR
HMM! i DON'T LiKE THE LOOK OF THAT!!
..i SURE DON'T LiKE THE LOOK OF THAT!
..AND i DEFINiTELY DON'T LiKE THE LOOK OF THAT!
X-RAY
...WHAT DO i HAVE, DOCTOR? ..iS iT SERiOUS?
...OH, YOU'RE iN PERFECT HEALTH. ..i JUST DON'T LiKE YOUR LOOKS!

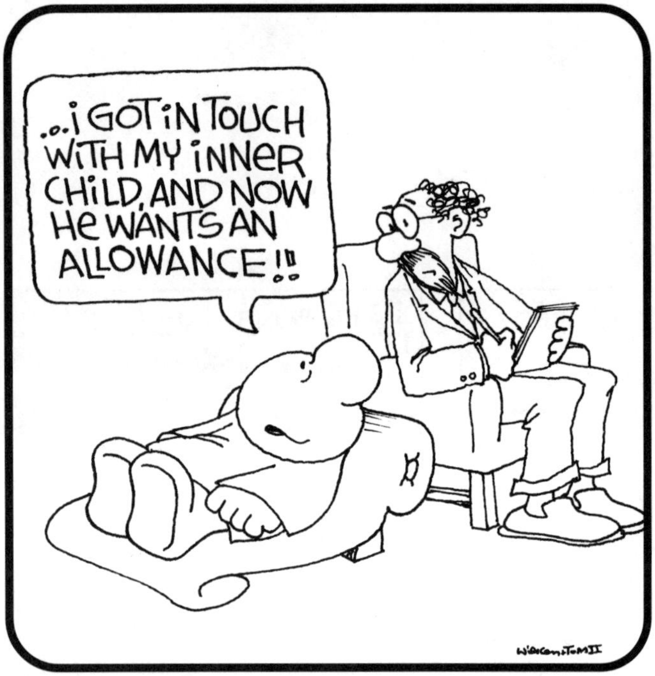
..i GOT iN TOUCH WiTH MY iNNeR CHiLD, AND NOW He WANTS AN ALLOWANCE!!

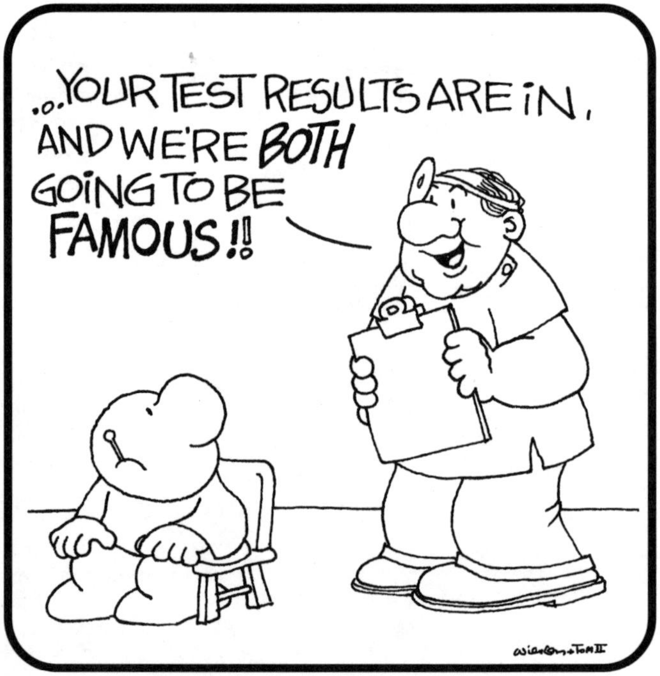
..YOUR TEST RESULTS ARE iN, AND WE'RE BOTH GOiNG TO BE FAMOUS!!

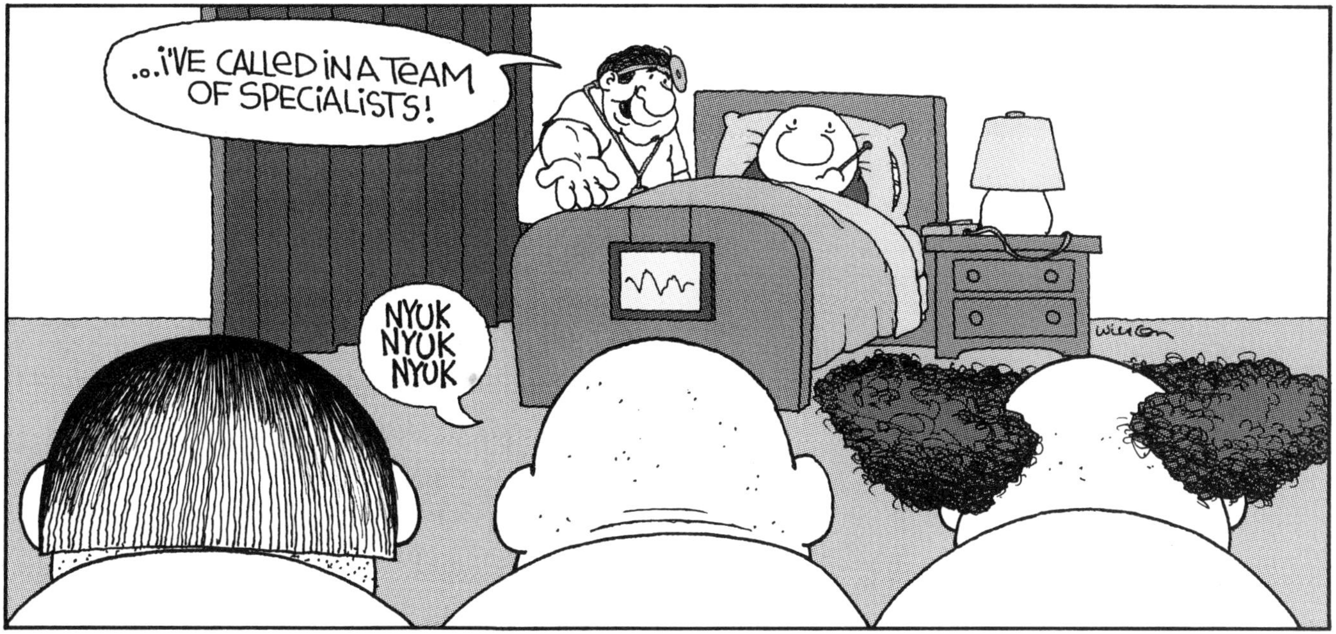
..○..I'VE CALLED IN A TEAM OF SPECIALISTS!
NYUK NYUK NYUK
WILSON

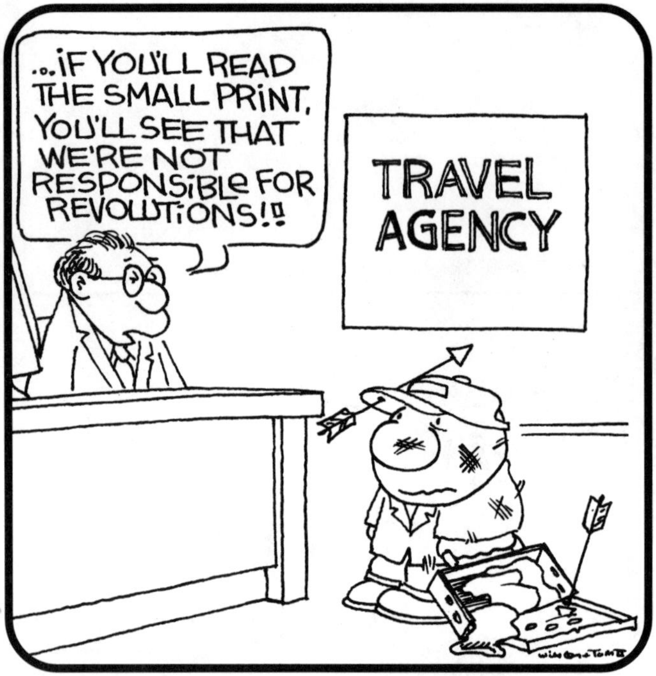
..IF YOU'LL READ THE SMALL PRINT, YOU'LL SEE THAT WE'RE NOT RESPONSIBLE FOR REVOLUTIONS!!
TRAVEL AGENCY

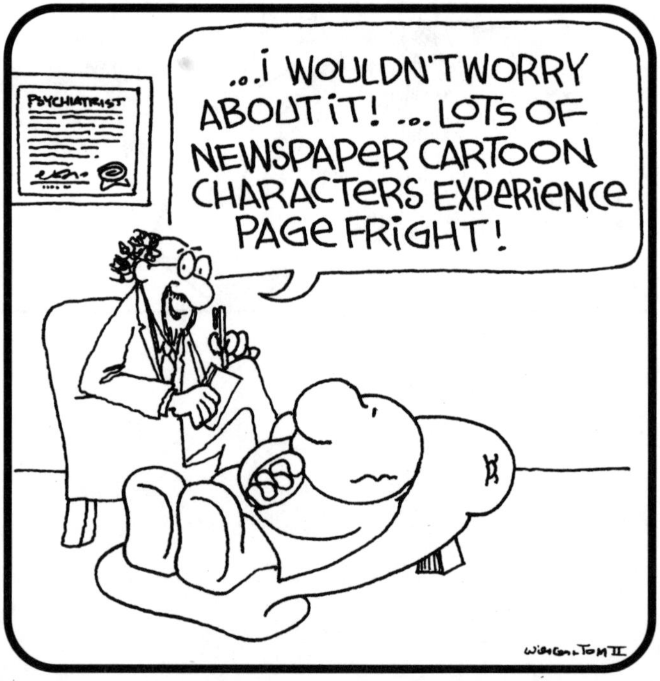
PSYCHIATRIST
..I WOULDN'T WORRY ABOUT IT! ..LOTS OF NEWSPAPER CARTOON CHARACTERS EXPERIENCE PAGE FRIGHT!

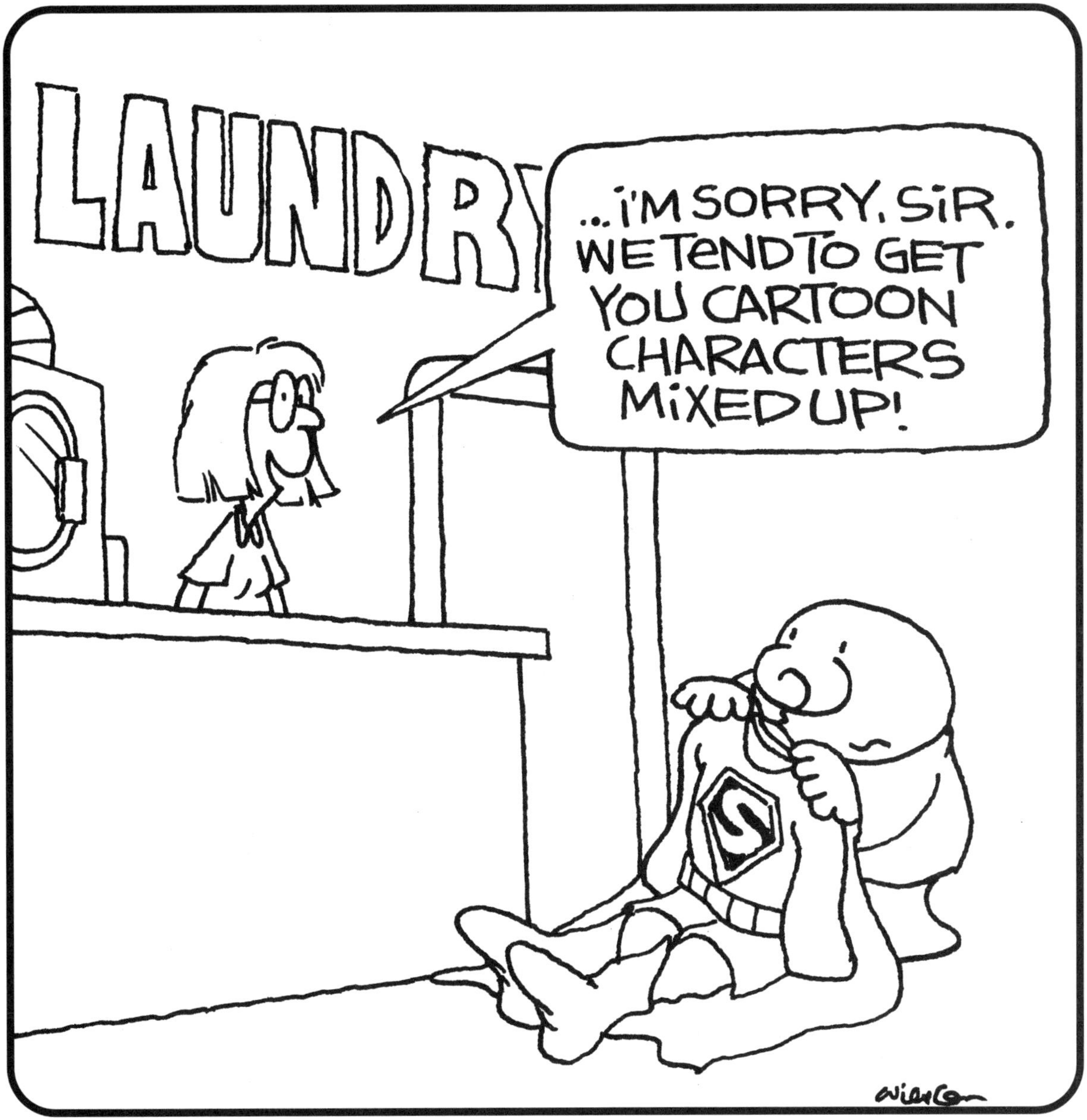
LAUNDRY
...I'M SORRY, SIR. WE TEND TO GET YOU CARTOON CHARACTERS MIXED UP!

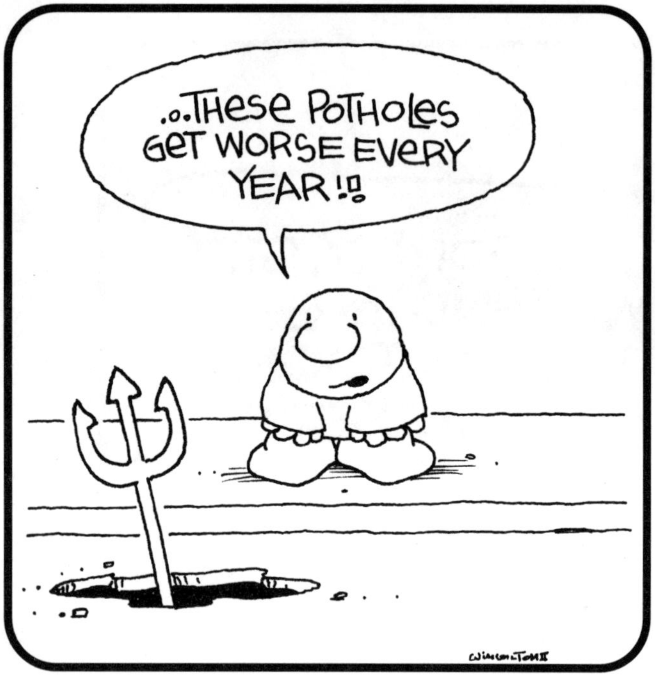
..o.THESE POTHOLES GET WORSE EVERY YEAR!!

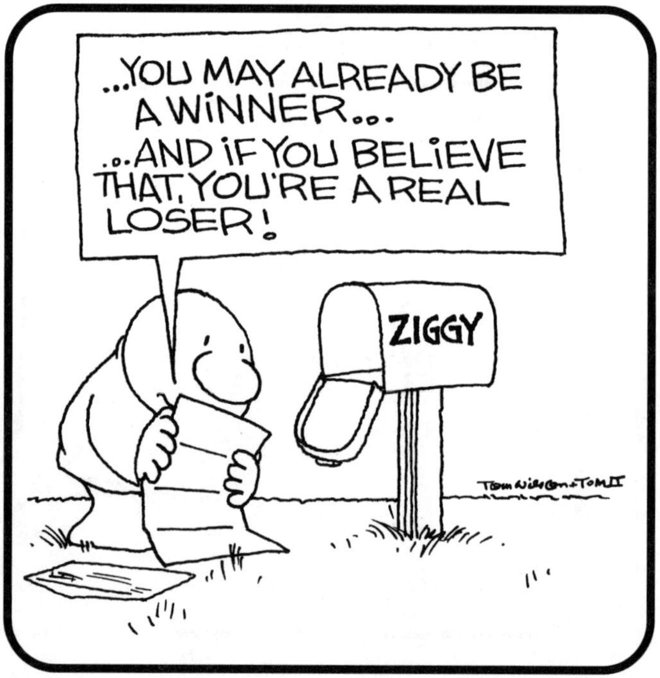
...YOU MAY ALREADY BE A WINNER...
..o.AND IF YOU BELIEVE THAT, YOU'RE A REAL LOSER!
ZIGGY

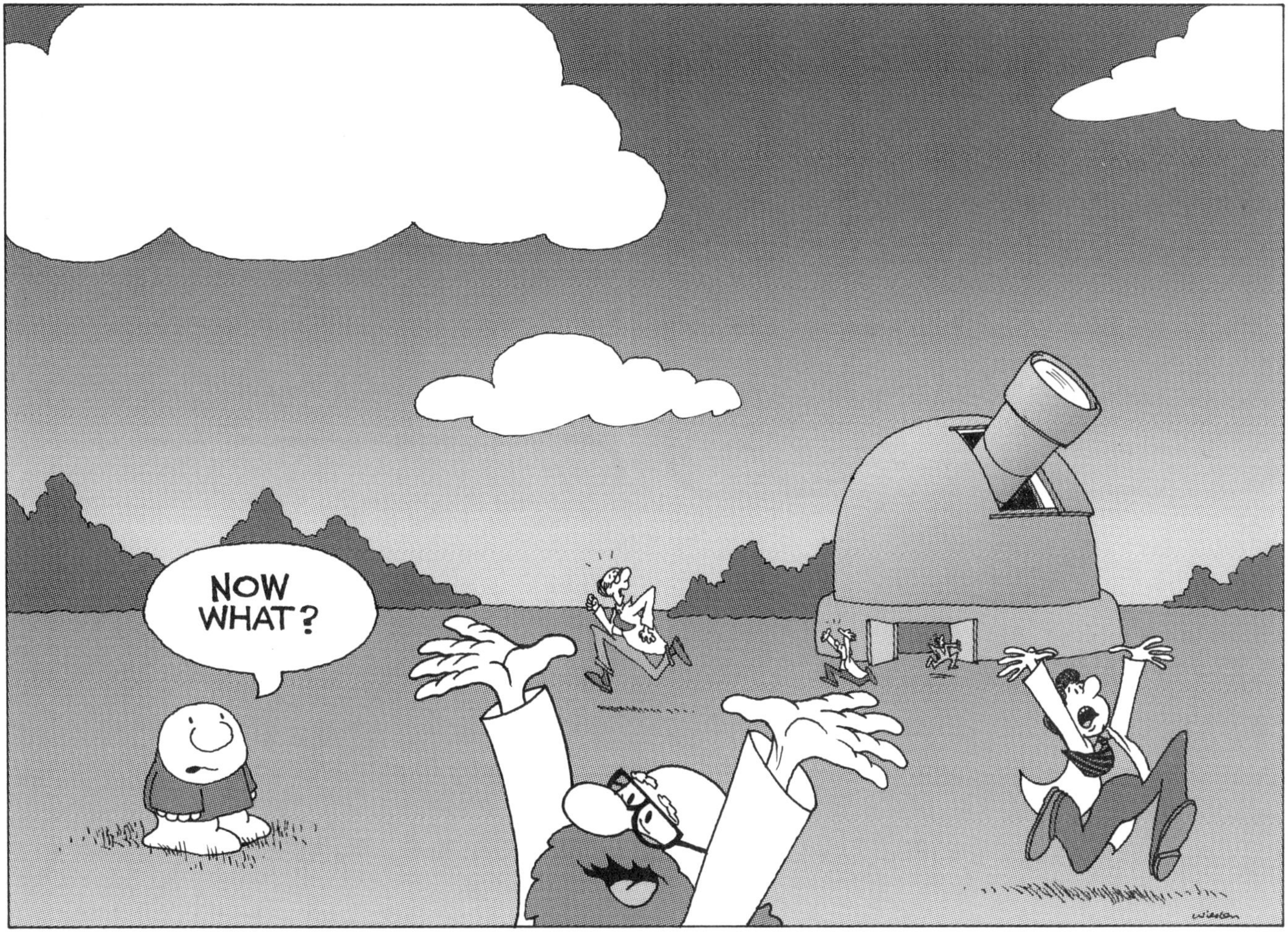
NOW WHAT?

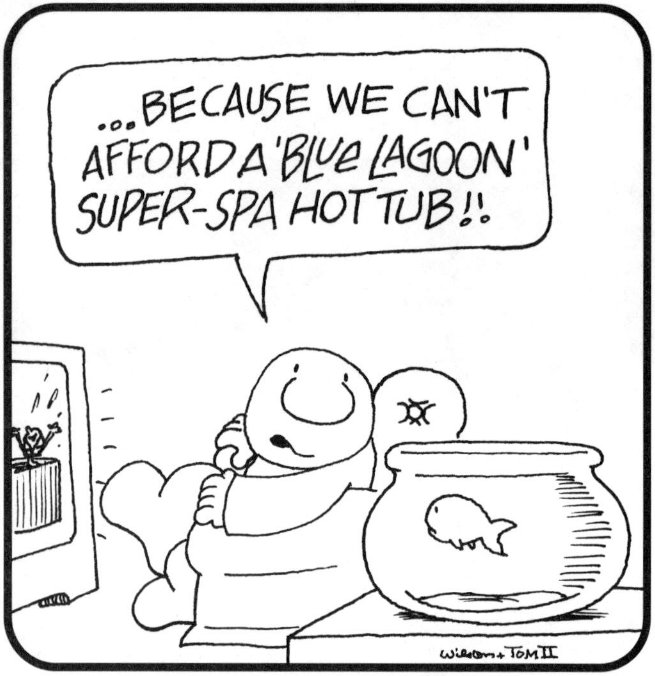
...BECAUSE WE CAN'T AFFORD A 'BLUE LAGOON' SUPER-SPA HOT TUB!!
Wilson+TOM II

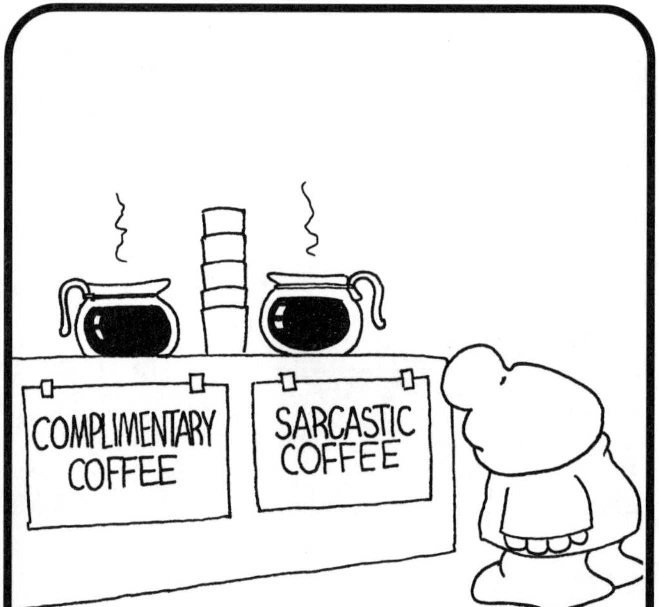
COMPLIMENTARY COFFEE
SARCASTIC COFFEE
Wilson+TOM II

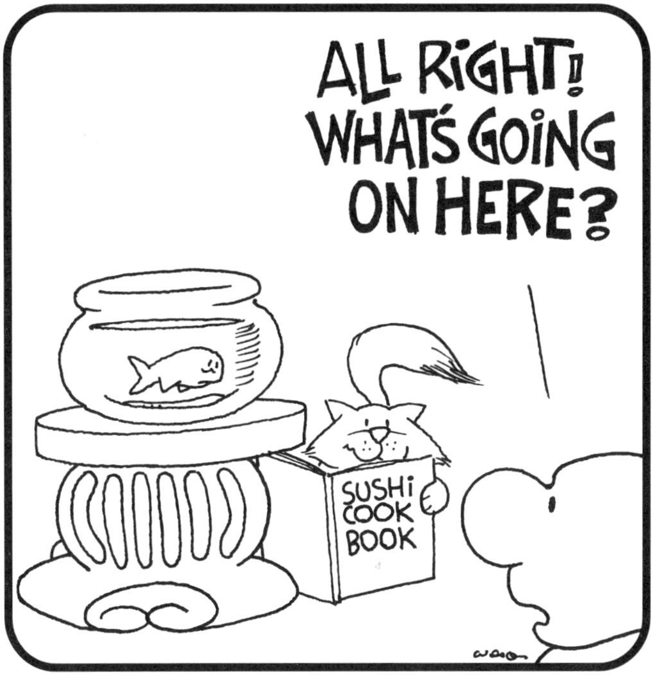
ALL RIGHT!
WHAT'S GOING
ON HERE?
SUSHI
COOK
BOOK

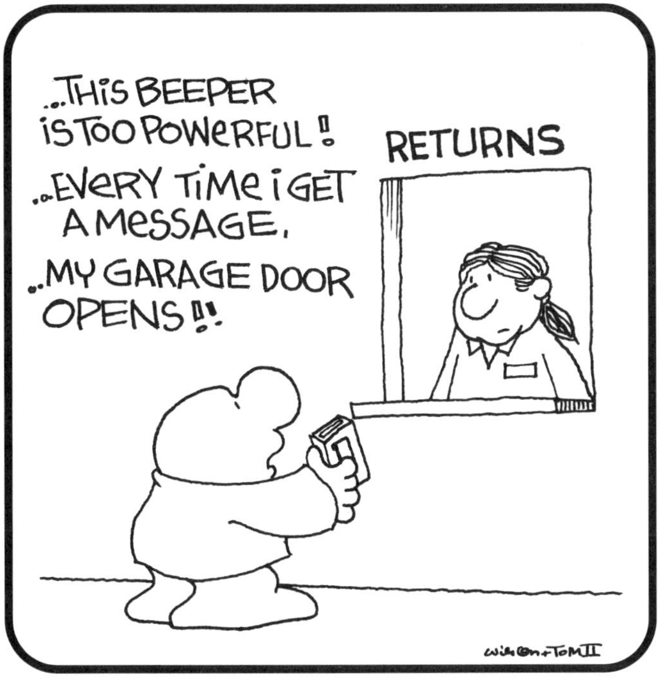
..THIS BEEPER
IS TOO POWERFUL!
..EVERY TIME I GET
A MESSAGE,
..MY GARAGE DOOR
OPENS!!
RETURNS

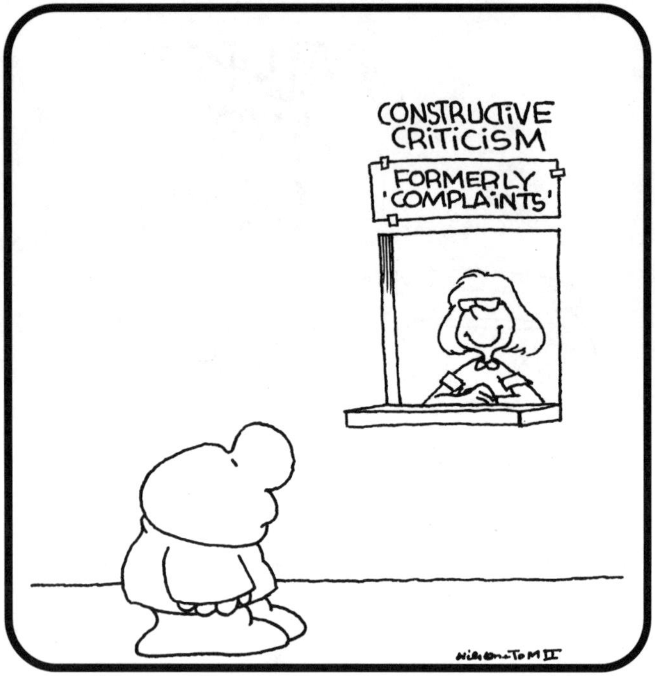
CONSTRUCTIVE CRITICISM
FORMERLY 'COMPLAINTS'

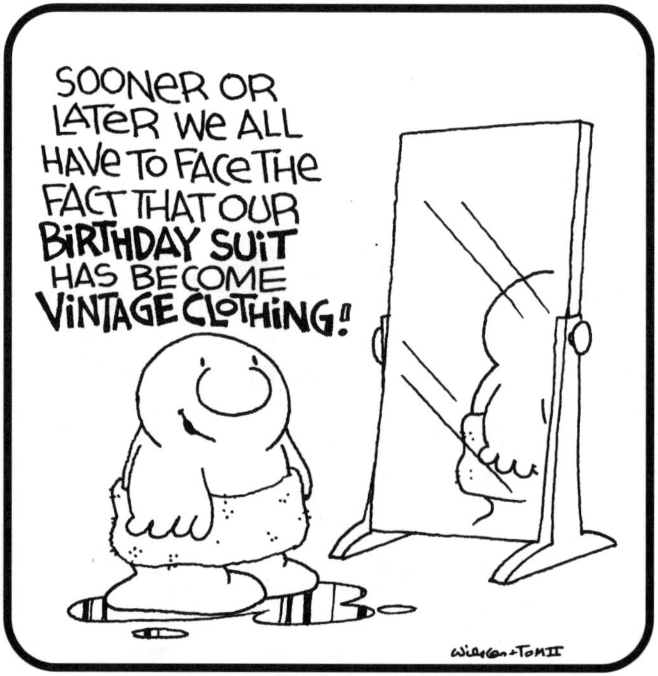
SOONER OR LATER WE ALL HAVE TO FACE THE FACT THAT OUR BIRTHDAY SUIT HAS BECOME VINTAGE CLOTHING!

TV USED TO BE ALL ABOUT 'ESCAPISM'..STORIES YOU'D NEVER ENCOUNTER IN YOUR OWN LIFE.
..NOW, IT'S ALL THIS REALITY-BASED STUFF...
...ORDINARY PEOPLE ON TALK SHOWS AND GAME SHOWS ..STUCK ON ISLANDS AND IN HOUSES AND CAUGHT ON HIDDEN CAMERA.
...WHAT DO YOU HAVE TO DO TO ENJOY A LITTLE ESCAPISM THESE DAYS?

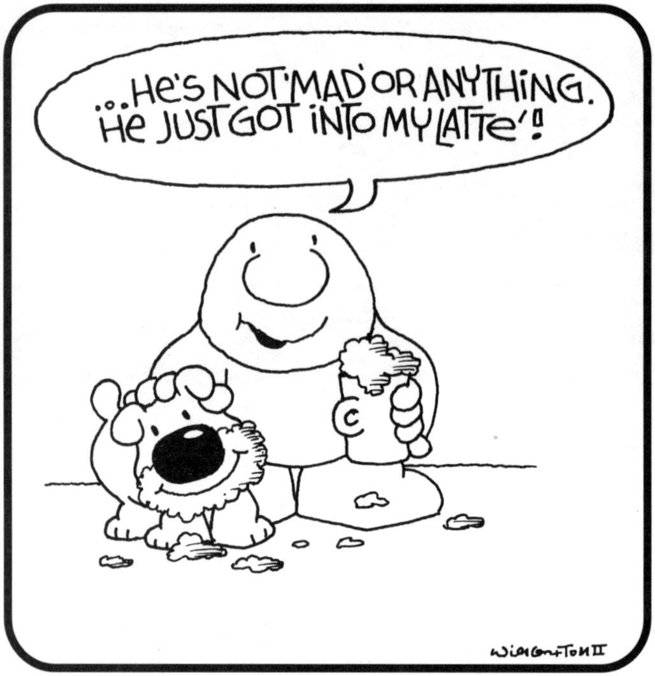
...HE'S NOT 'MAD' OR ANYTHING. HE JUST GOT INTO MY LATTE'!
WILDER-TOM II

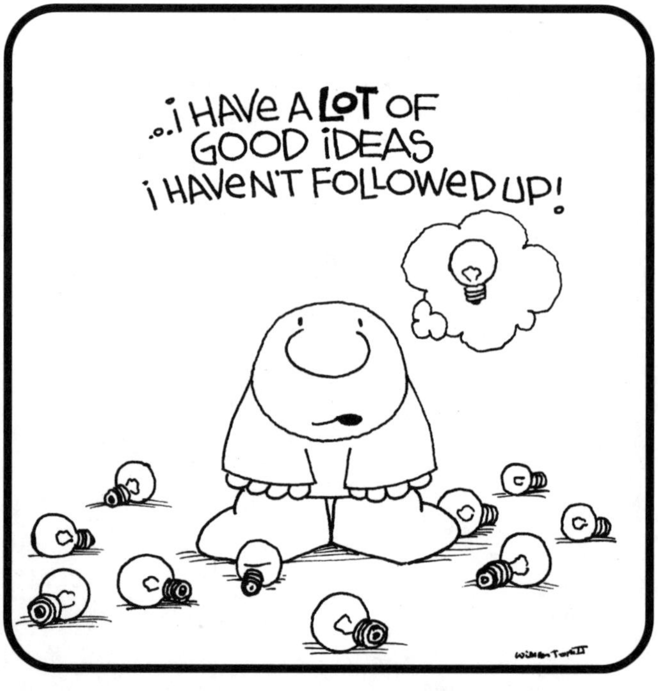
...I HAVE A LOT OF GOOD IDEAS I HAVEN'T FOLLOWED UP!
WILDER-TOM II

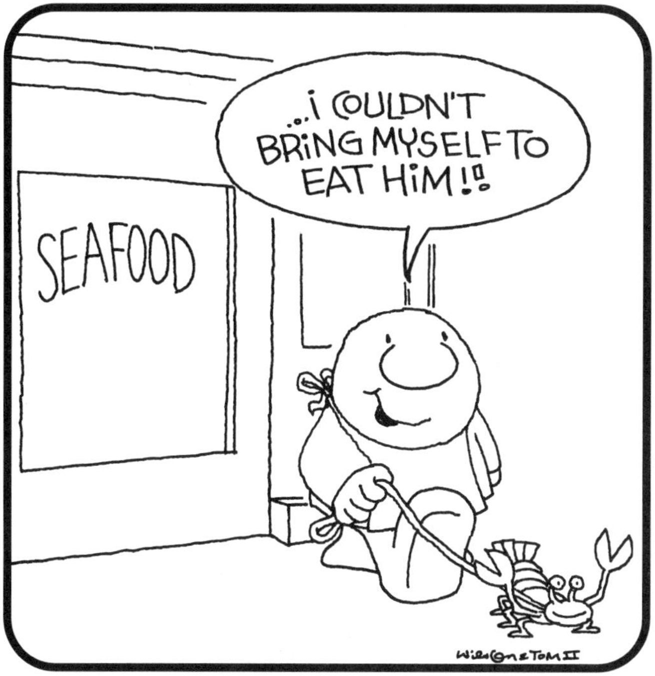

SEAFOOD
...I COULDN'T BRING MYSELF TO EAT HIM!!

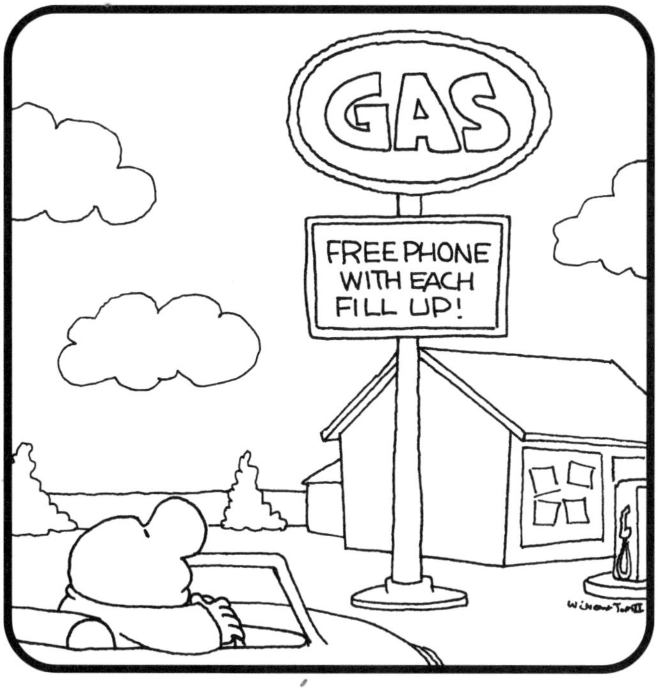

GAS
FREE PHONE WITH EACH FILL UP!

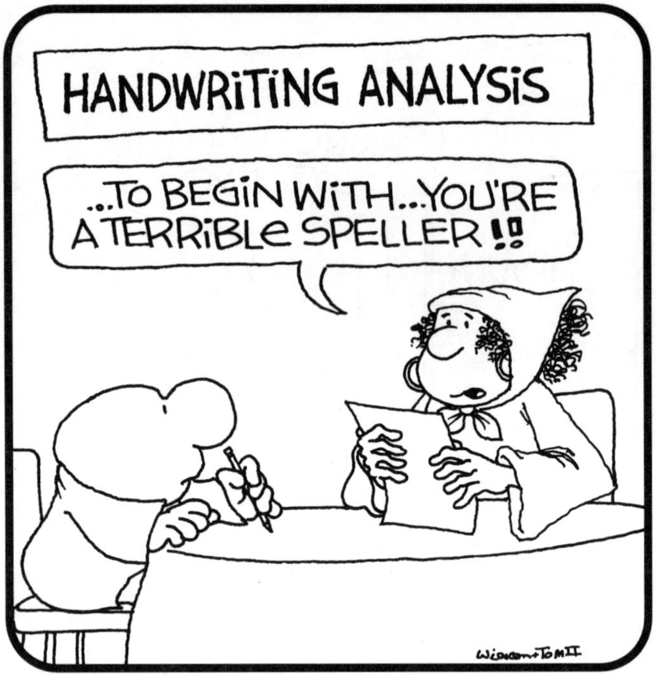
HANDWRITING ANALYSIS
...TO BEGIN WITH...YOU'RE A TERRIBLE SPELLER!!
WILSON + TOM II

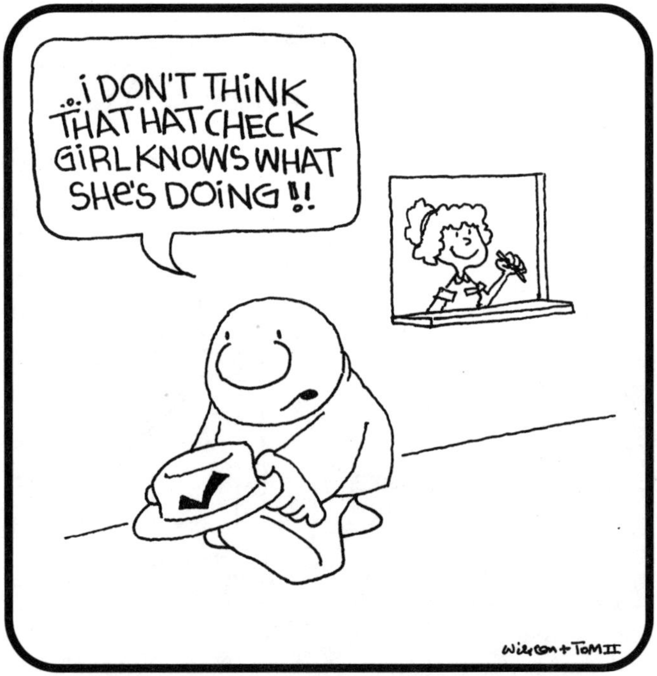
...I DON'T THINK THAT HAT CHECK GIRL KNOWS WHAT SHE'S DOING!!
WILSON + TOM II

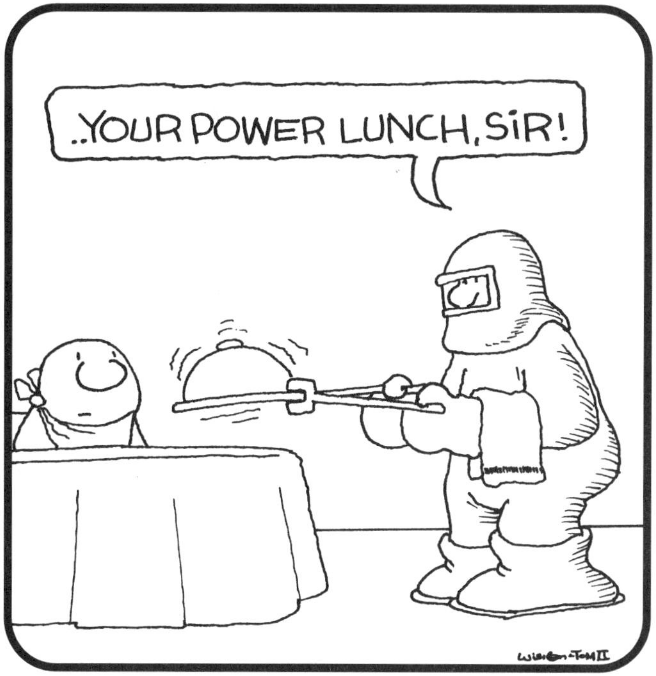
..YOUR POWER LUNCH, SIR!
WILSON-TOM II

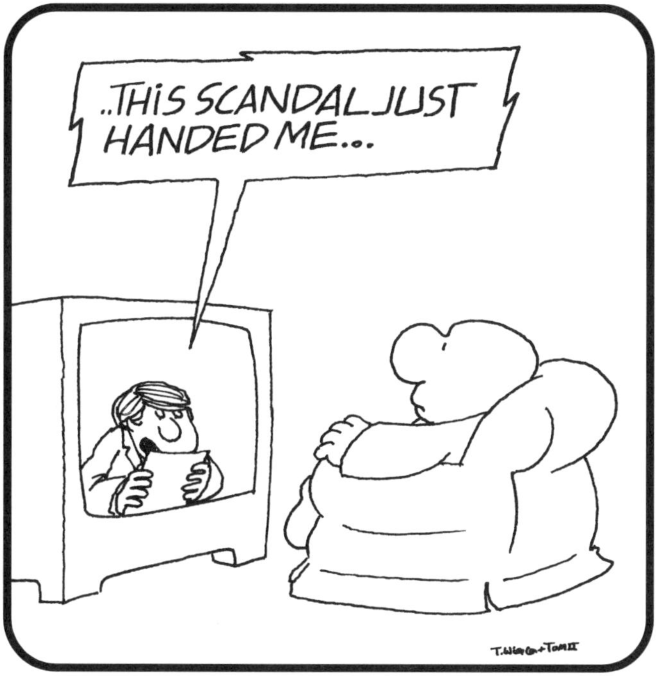
..THIS SCANDAL JUST HANDED ME...
T.WILSON+TOM II

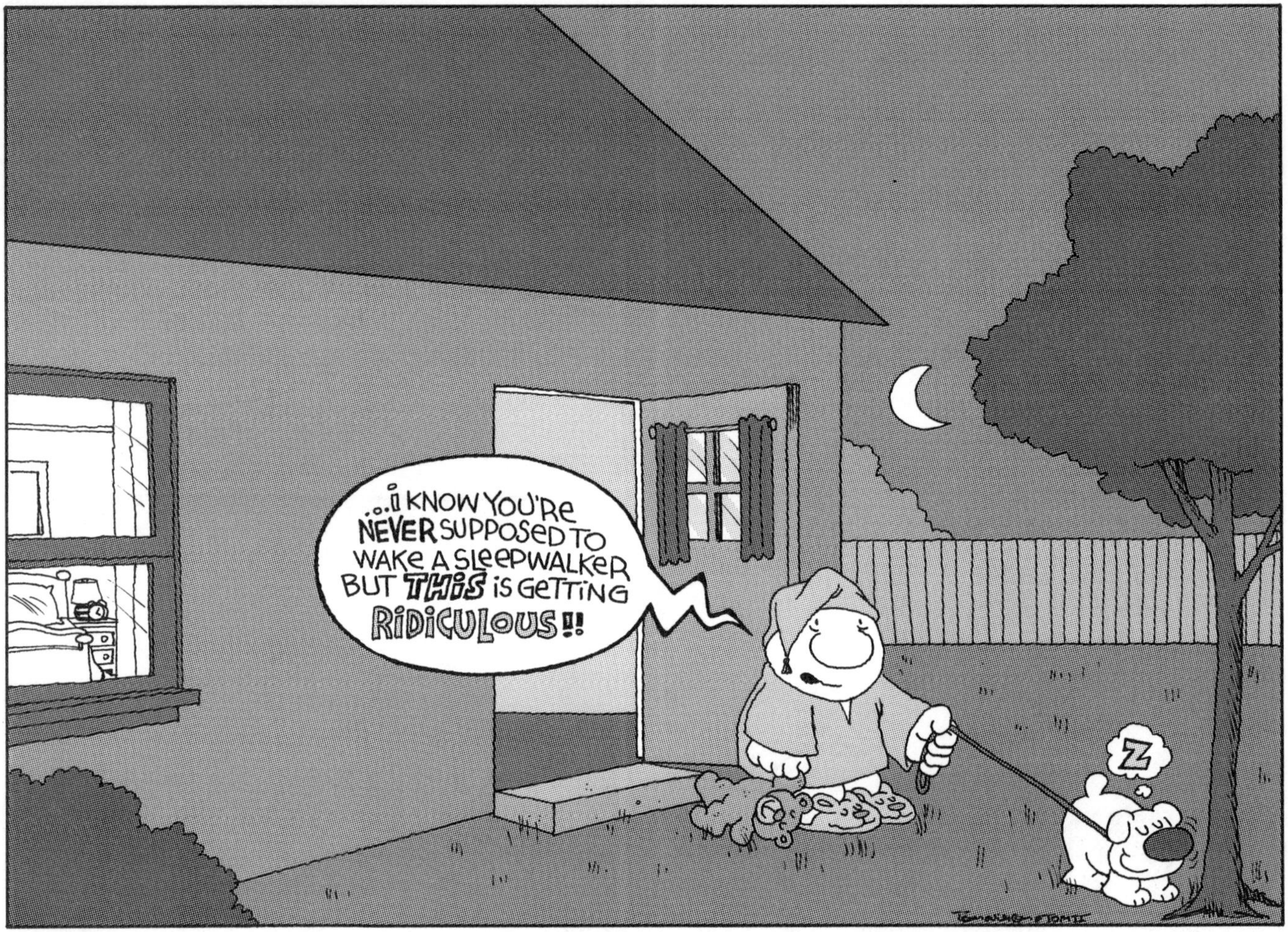
...I KNOW YOU'RE NEVER SUPPOSED TO WAKE A SLEEPWALKER BUT THIS IS GETTING RIDICULOUS!!
Z

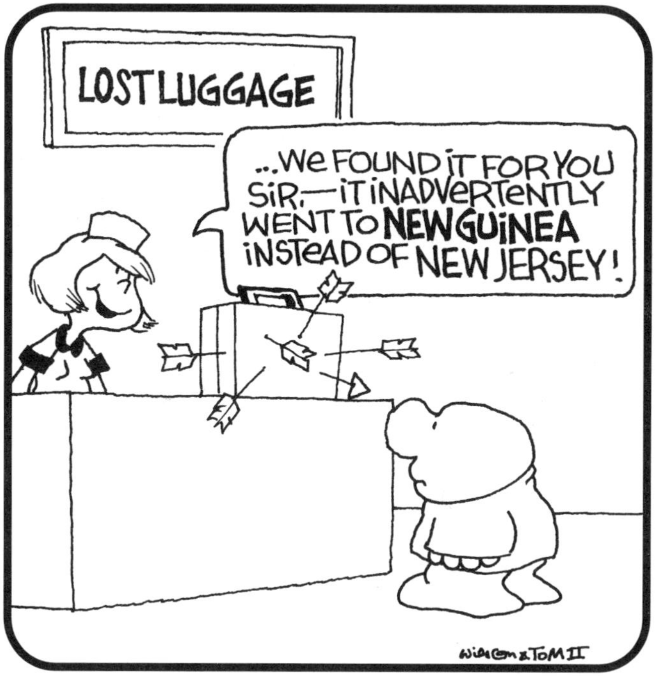
LOST LUGGAGE
...WE FOUND IT FOR YOU SIR,—IT INADVERTENTLY WENT TO NEW GUINEA INSTEAD OF NEW JERSEY!
Wildcon & TOM II

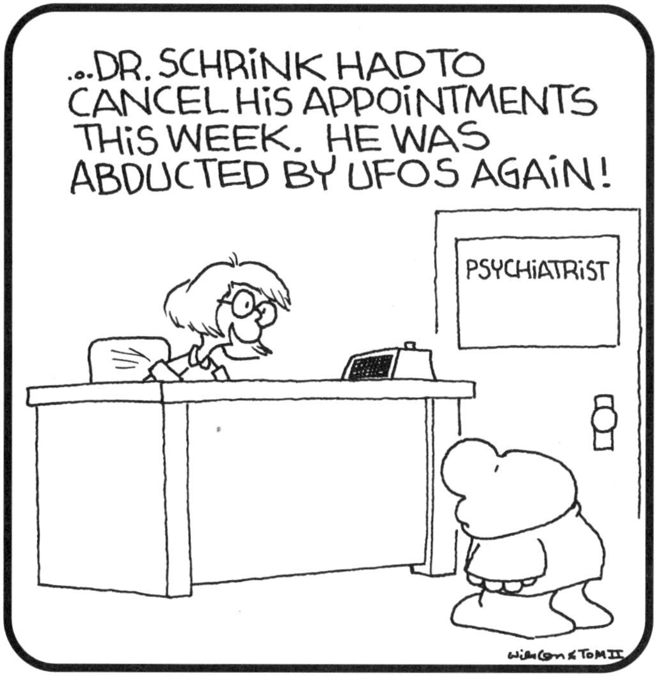
...DR. SCHRINK HAD TO CANCEL HIS APPOINTMENTS THIS WEEK. HE WAS ABDUCTED BY UFOS AGAIN!
PSYCHIATRIST
Wildcon & TOM II

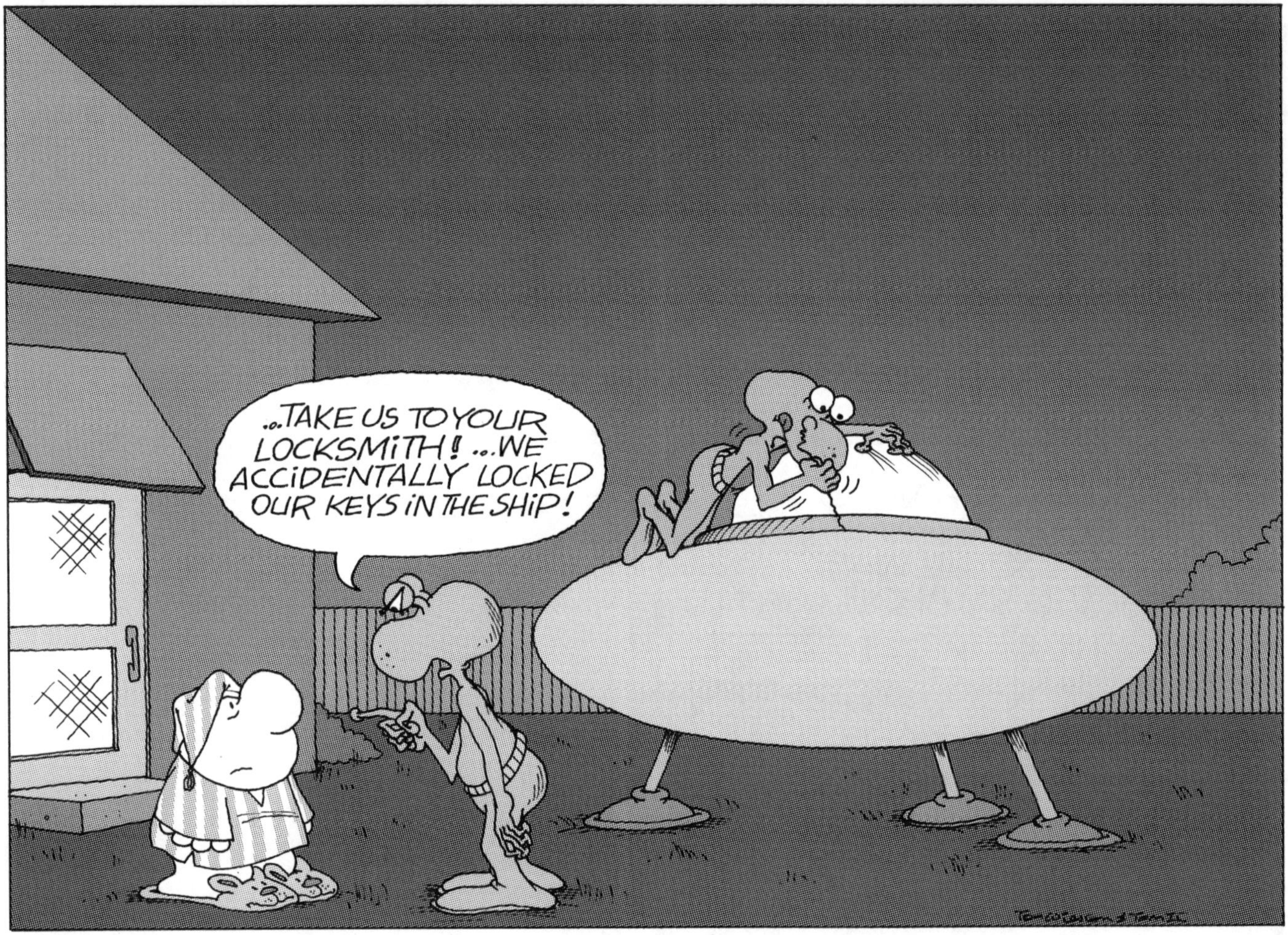
..TAKE US TO YOUR LOCKSMITH! ...WE ACCIDENTALLY LOCKED OUR KEYS IN THE SHIP!

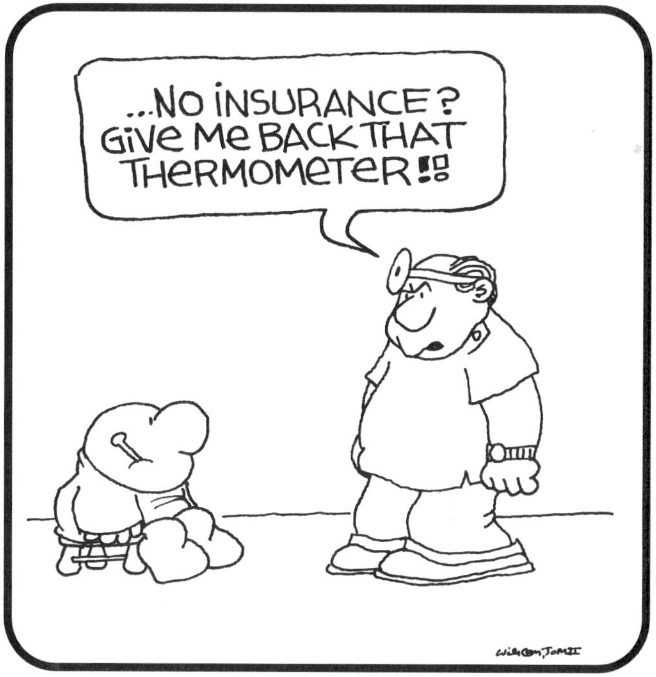
...NO INSURANCE? GIVE ME BACK THAT THERMOMETER!?

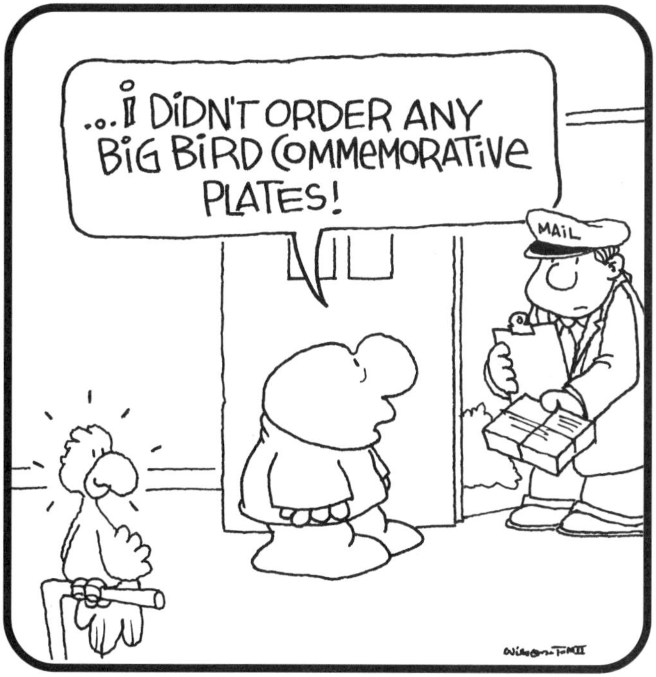
...I DIDN'T ORDER ANY BIG BIRD COMMEMORATIVE PLATES!
MAIL

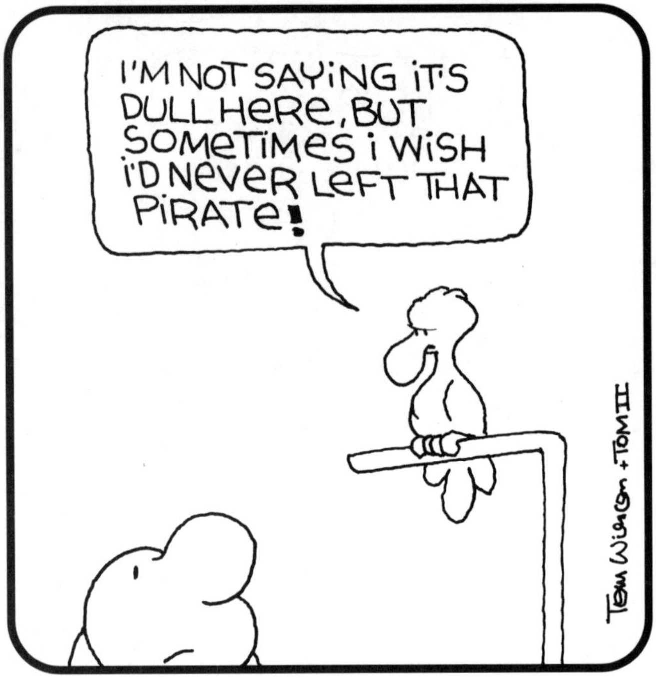
I'M NOT SAYING IT'S DULL HERE, BUT SOMETIMES I WISH I'D NEVER LEFT THAT PIRATE!
TOM WILSON + TOM II

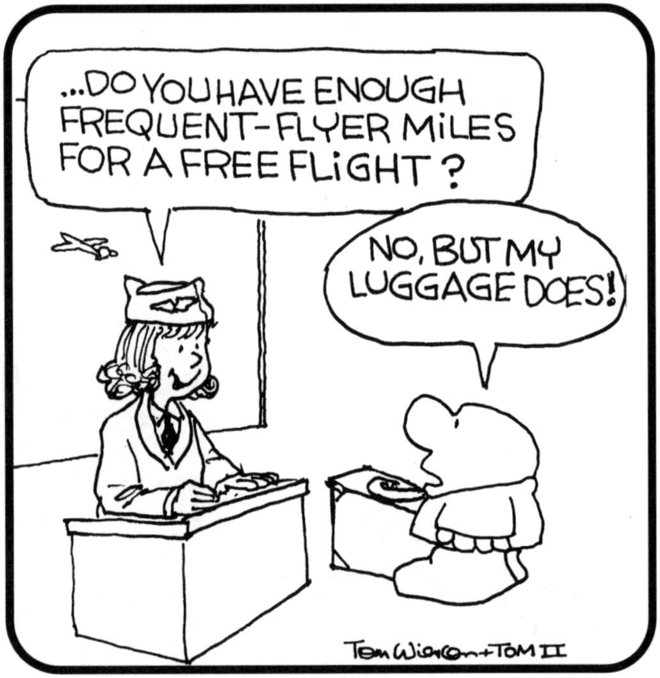
...DO YOU HAVE ENOUGH FREQUENT-FLYER MILES FOR A FREE FLIGHT?
NO, BUT MY LUGGAGE DOES!
TOM WILSON + TOM II

..HERE'S YOUR RECEIPT, SIR! ..HAVE A NICE DAY!!
...EVERYONE OUT TODAY SURE IS FRIENDLY... I SHOULD WALK TO THE MARKET MORE OFTEN!

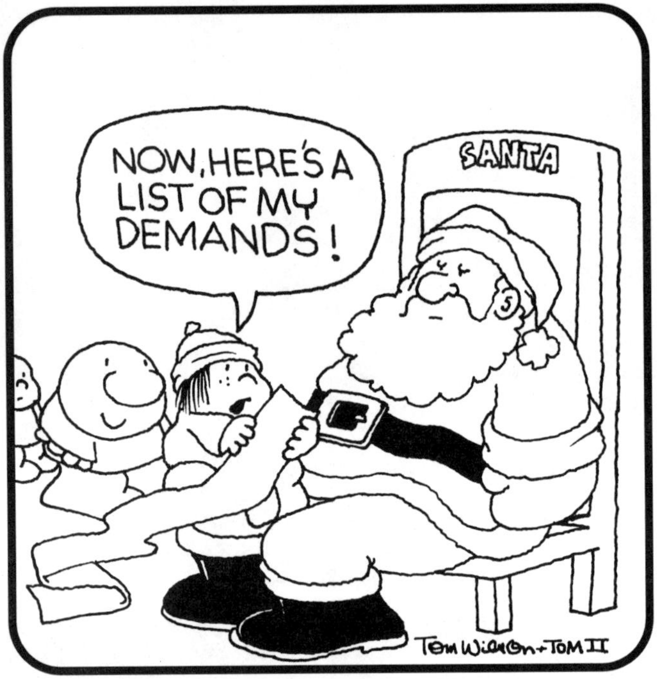
NOW, HERE'S A LIST OF MY DEMANDS!
SANTA
TOM WILSON + TOM II

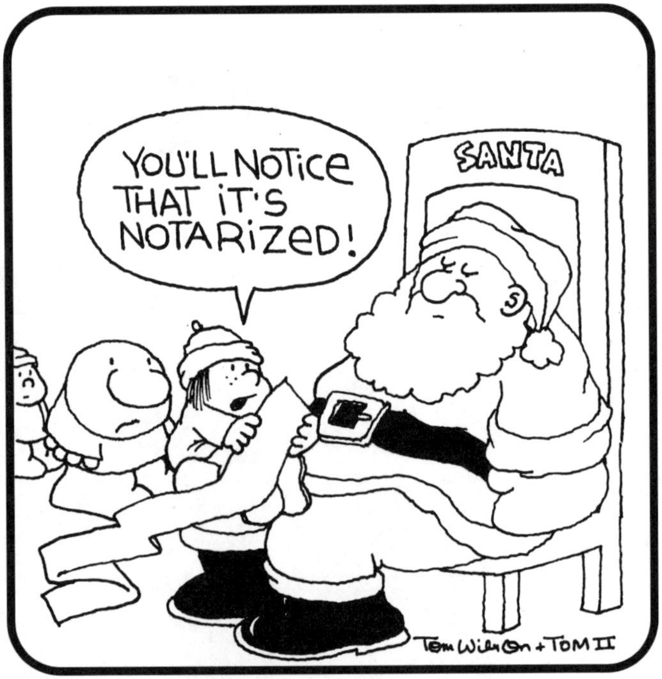
YOU'LL NOTICE THAT IT'S NOTARIZED!
SANTA
TOM WILSON + TOM II

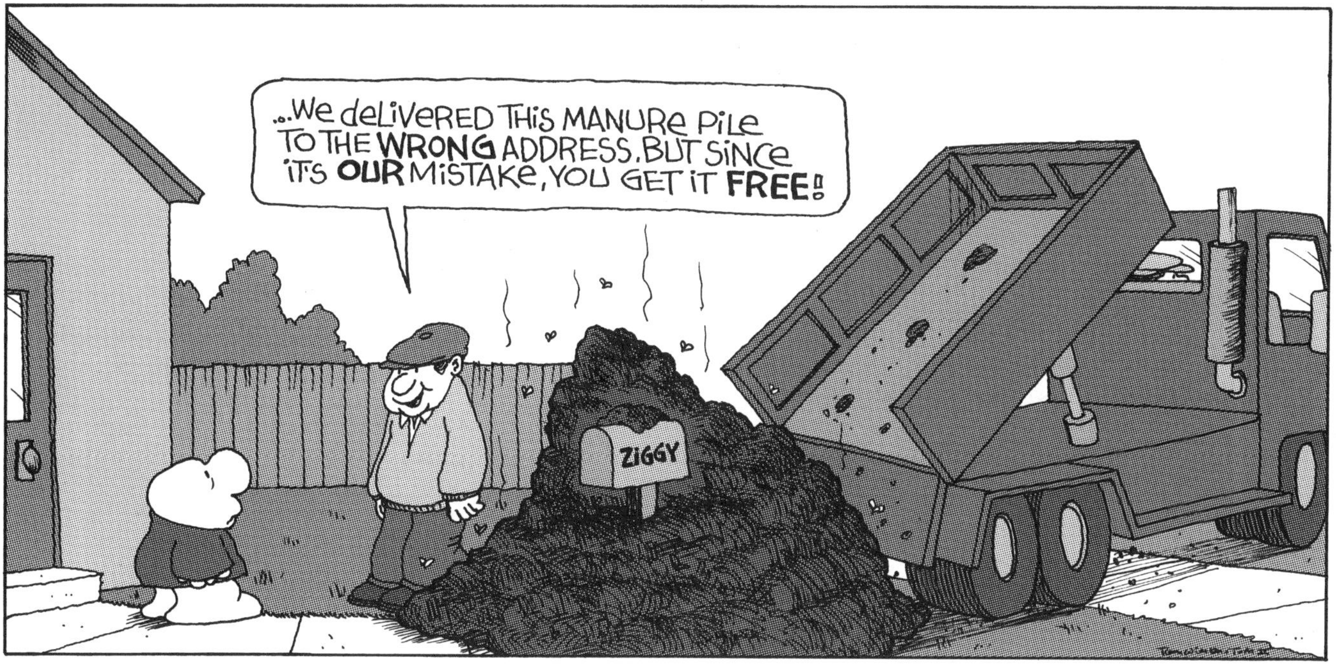
...We delivered THIS MANURE PILE TO THE WRONG ADDRESS. BUT SINCE IT'S OUR MISTAKE, YOU GET IT FREE!!
ZIGGY

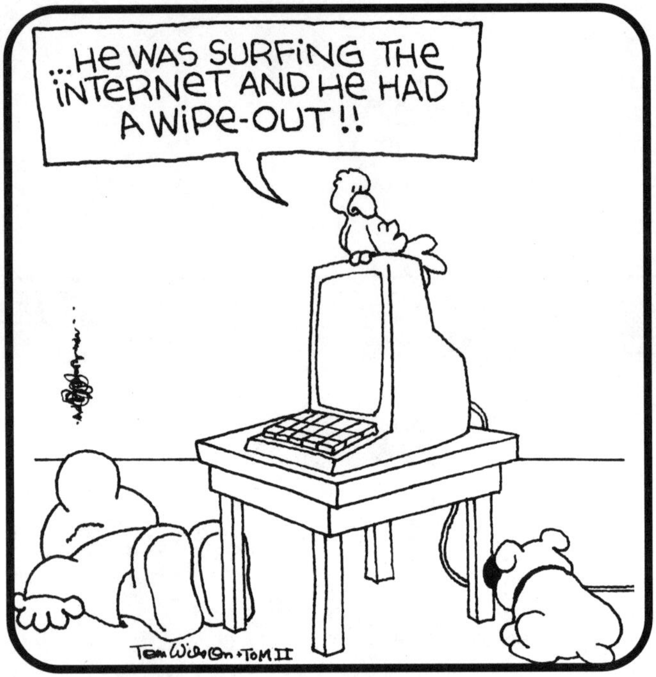
...HE WAS SURFING THE INTERNET AND HE HAD A WIPE-OUT!!
Tom Wilson + TOM II

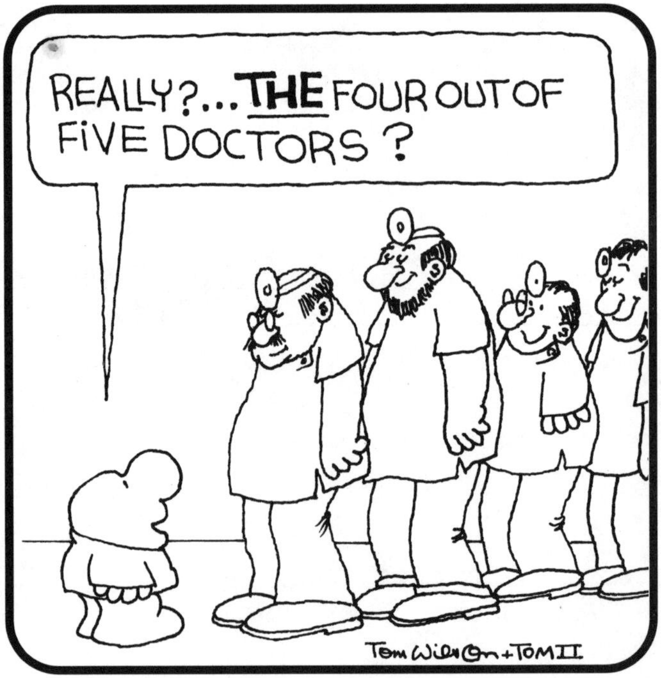
REALLY?... THE FOUR OUT OF FIVE DOCTORS ?
Tom Wilson + TOM II

..SOME PEOPLE SAY YOU SHOULD TREAT EACH DAY AS THE FIRST DAY OF THE REST OF YOUR LIFE!

..OTHERS PREFER TO APPROACH IT AS IF IT WERE THEIR LAST DAY ON EARTH!

..I TRIED TO FOLLOW THE BEST OF BOTH PHILOSOPHIES!!

..SO NOW I START EACH DAY NOT KNOWING WHETHER I'M COMING OR GOING!!

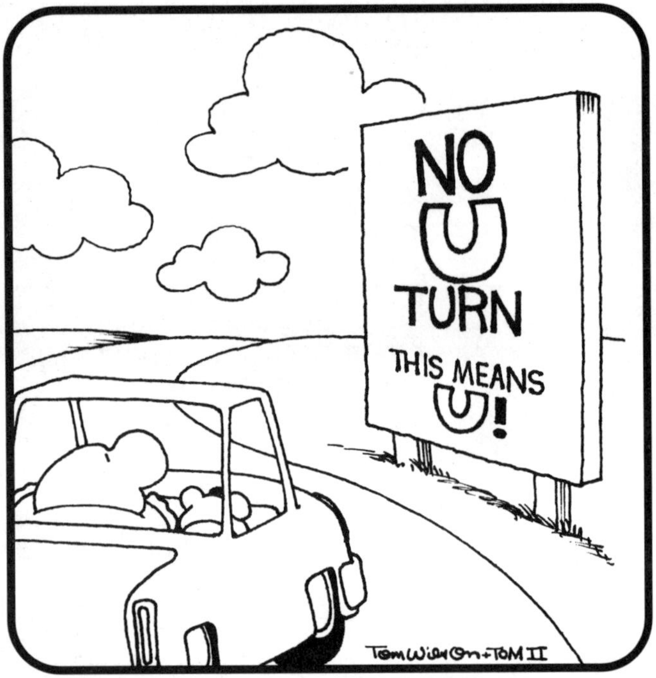
NO
U
TURN
THIS MEANS
U!
TOM WILSON + TOM II

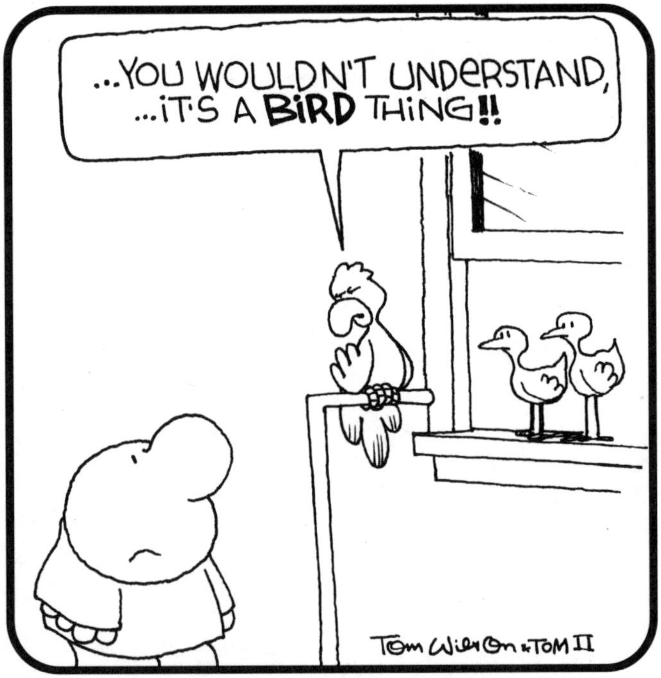
...YOU WOULDN'T UNDERSTAND,
...IT'S A **BIRD** THING!!
TOM WILSON + TOM II

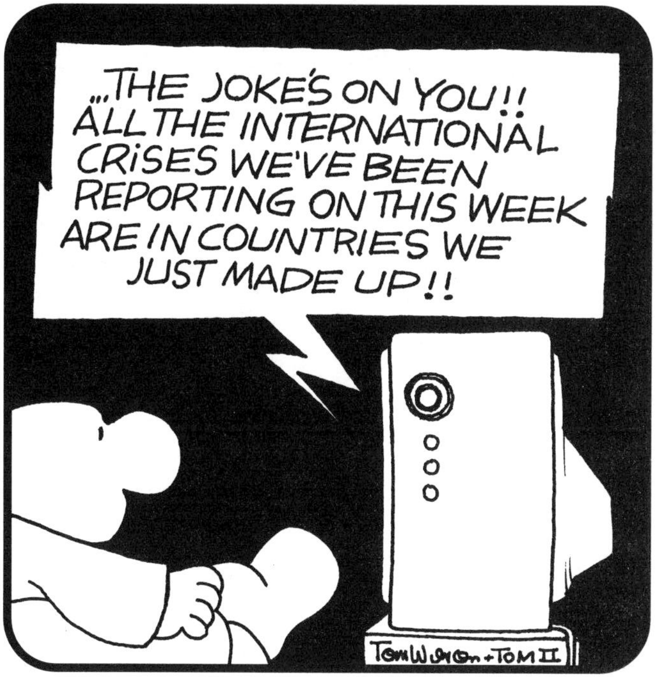
...THE JOKE'S ON YOU!! ALL THE INTERNATIONAL CRISES WE'VE BEEN REPORTING ON THIS WEEK ARE IN COUNTRIES WE JUST MADE UP!!
TOM WILSON + TOM II

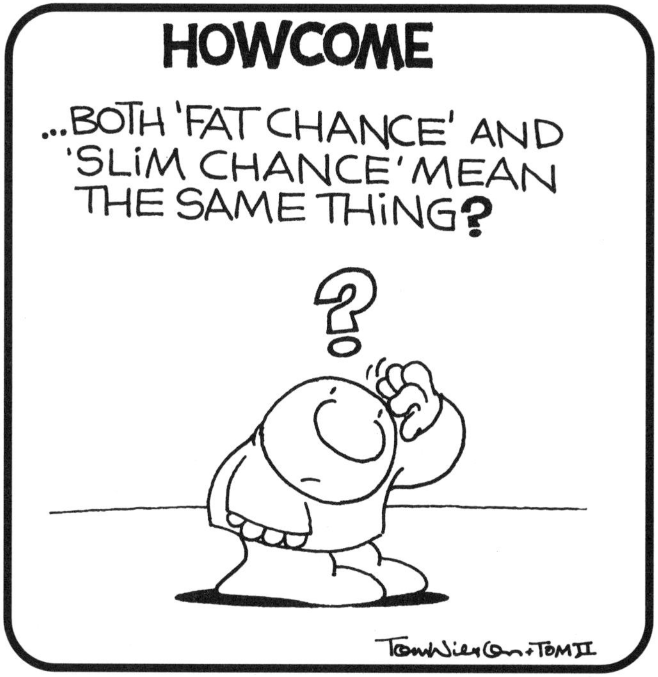
HOWCOME
...BOTH 'FAT CHANCE' AND 'SLIM CHANCE' MEAN THE SAME THING?
TOM WILSON + TOM II

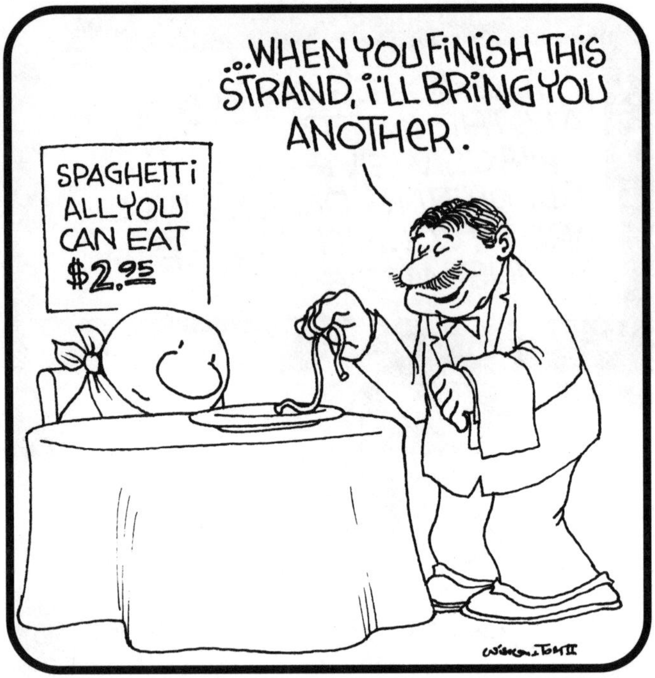
...WHEN YOU FINISH THIS STRAND, I'LL BRING YOU ANOTHER.
SPAGHETTI ALL YOU CAN EAT $2.95

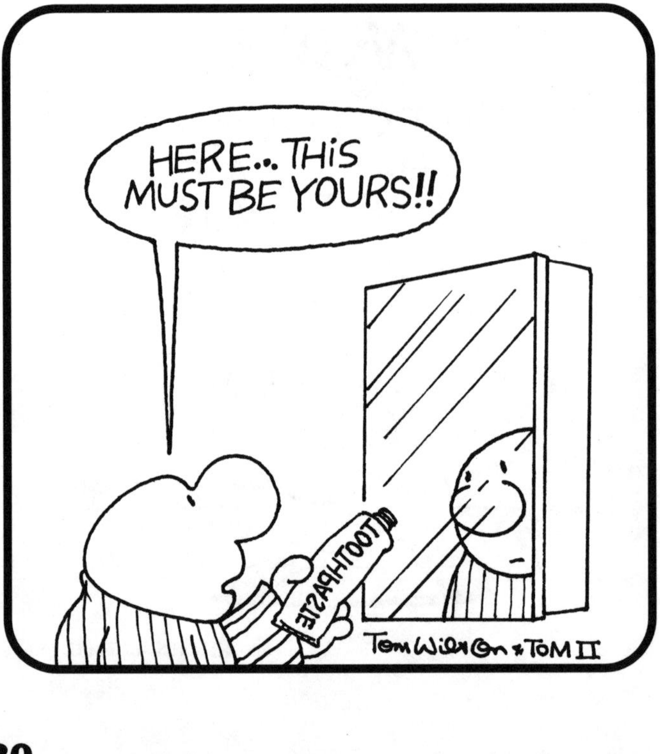
HERE... THIS MUST BE YOURS!!
TOOTHPASTE
TOM WILSON & TOM II

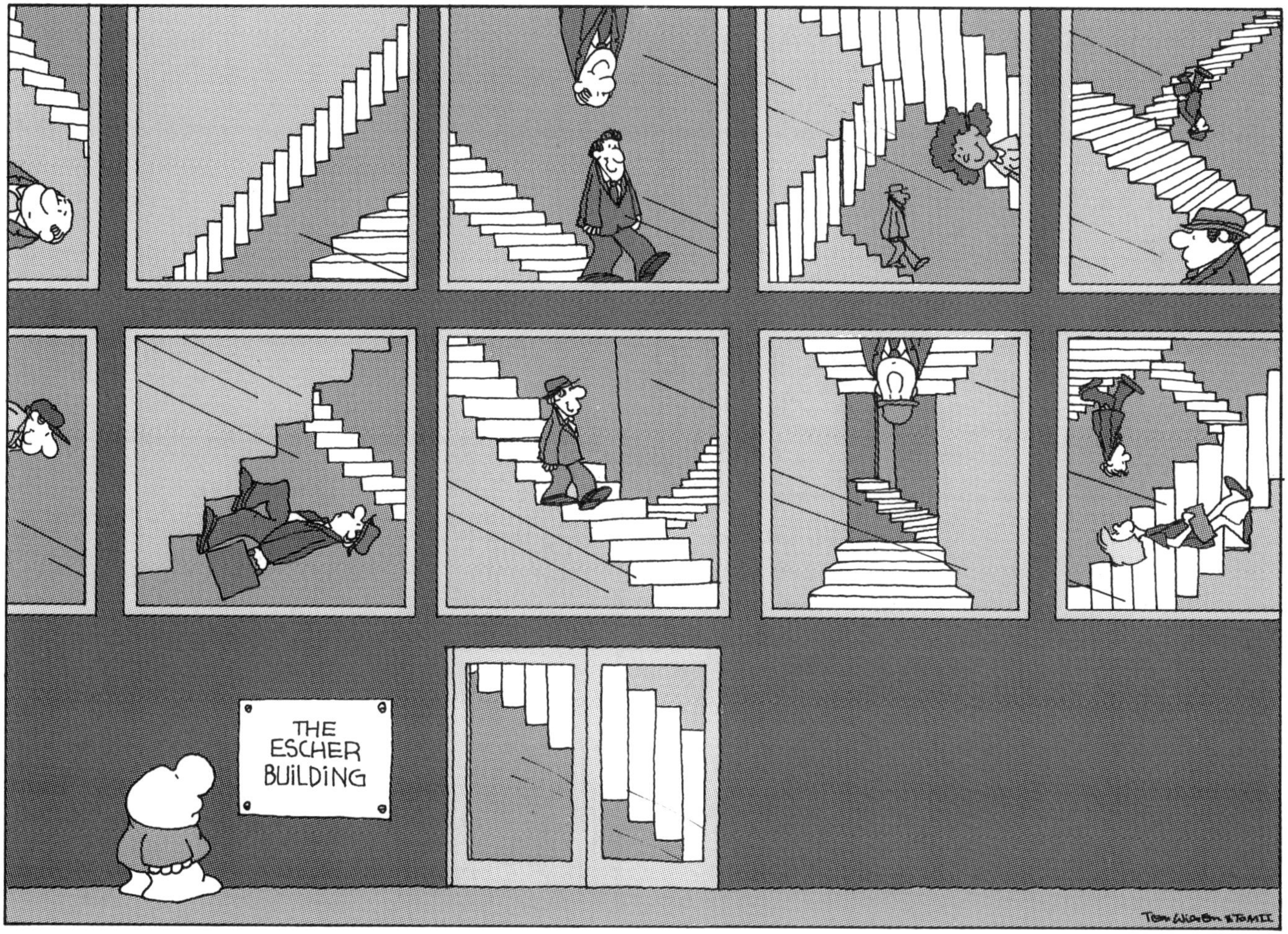
THE ESCHER BUILDING

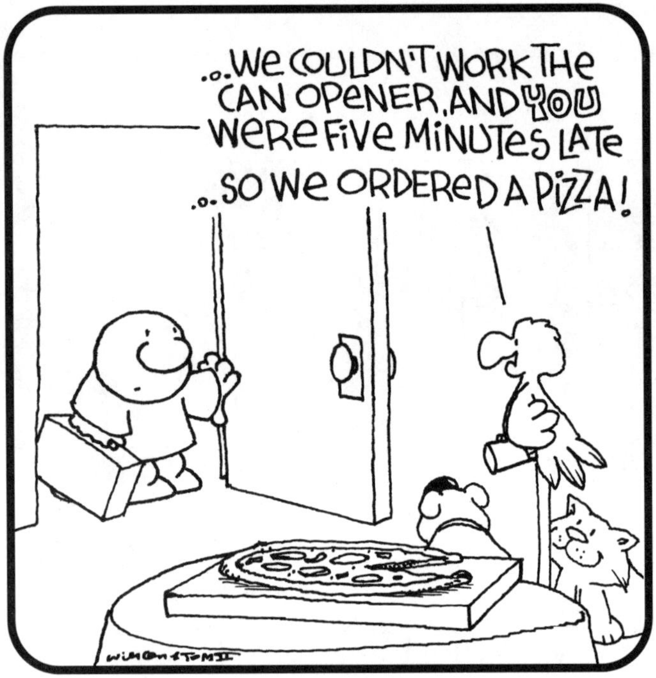
..WE COULDN'T WORK THE CAN OPENER, AND YOU WERE FIVE MINUTES LATE
..SO WE ORDERED A PIZZA!

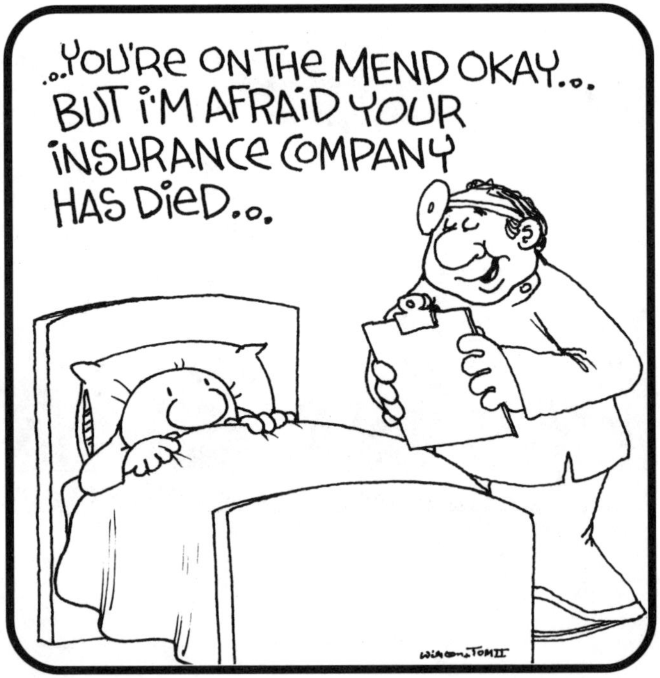
..YOU'RE ON THE MEND OKAY... BUT I'M AFRAID YOUR INSURANCE COMPANY HAS DIED...

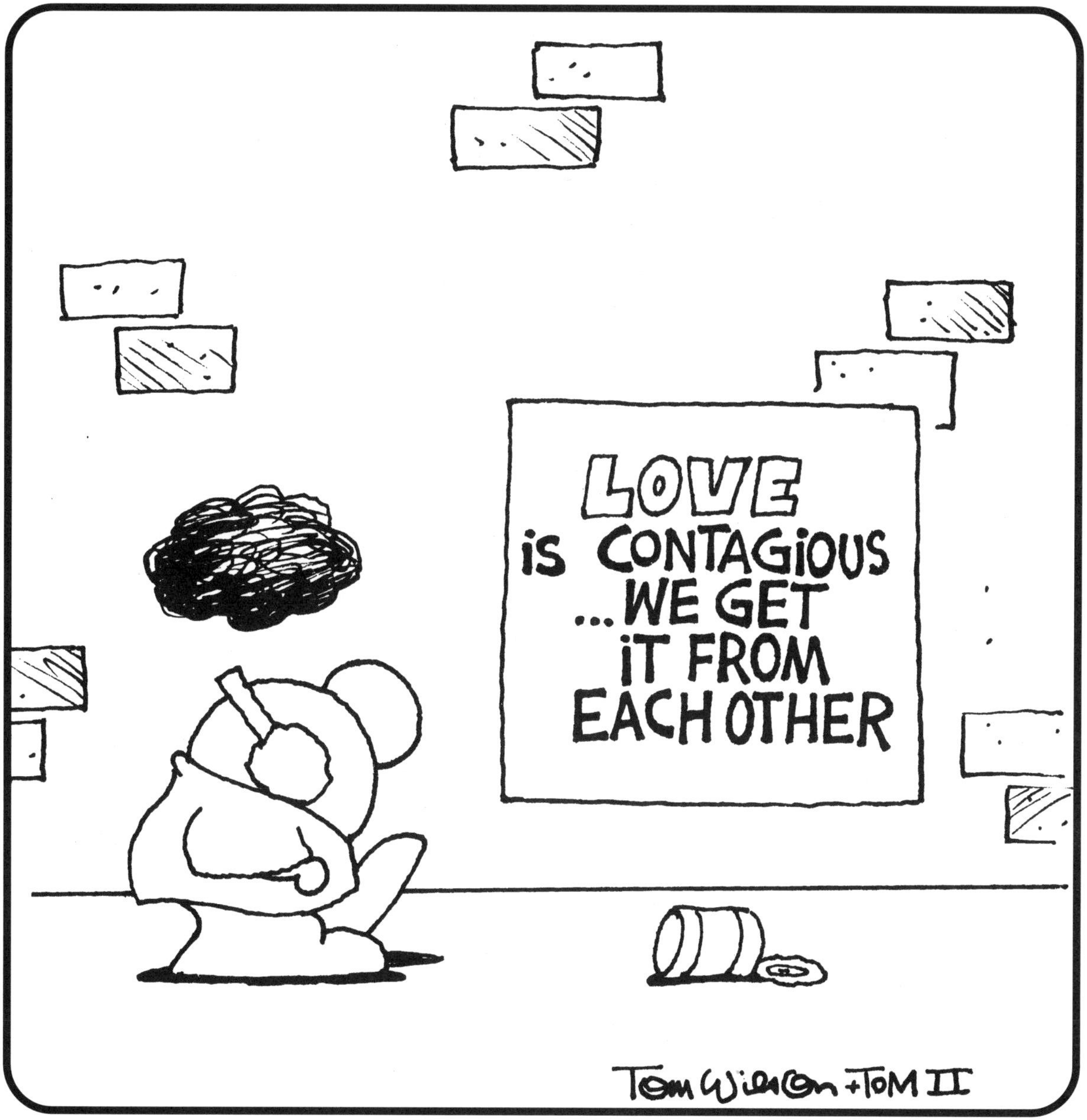
LOVE
is CONTAGIOUS
...WE GET
iT FROM
EACH OTHER
Tom Wilson + TOM II

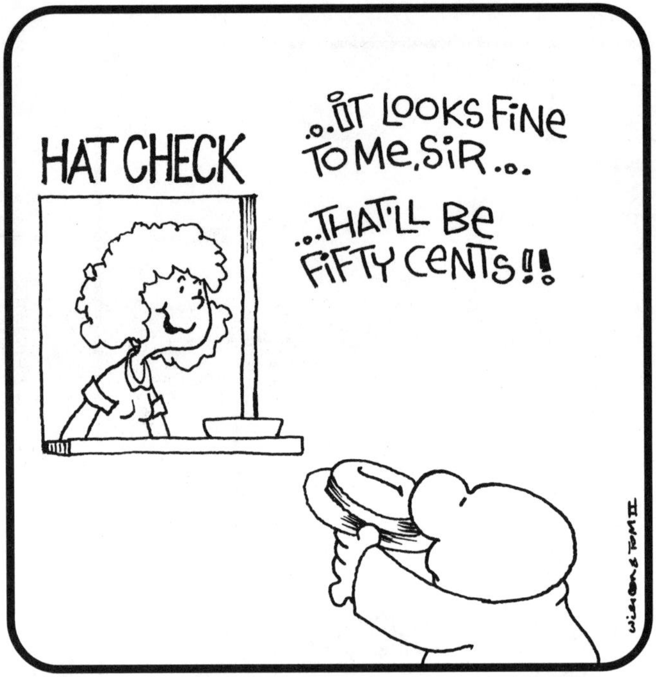
HAT CHECK
..IT LOOKS FINE TO ME, SIR...
..THAT'LL BE FIFTY CENTS!!

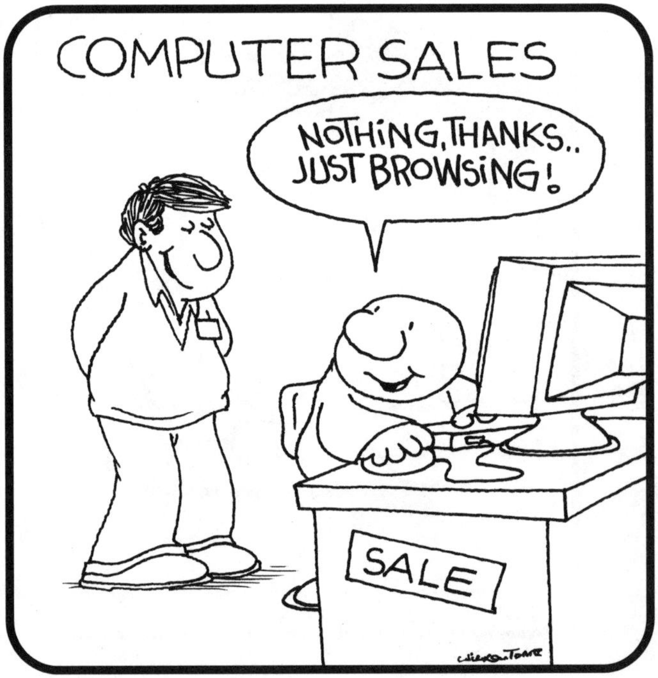
COMPUTER SALES
NOTHING, THANKS.. JUST BROWSING!
SALE

STARLIGHT... STARBRIGHT ...i WISH i MAY...i WISH i MIGHT HAVE THE WISH i WISH TONIGHT!!
PING!
WE WISH YOU A MERRY CHRISTMAS
WE WISH YOU A MERRY CHRISTMAS...
..FROM ZIGGY, TOM WILSON AND TOM II

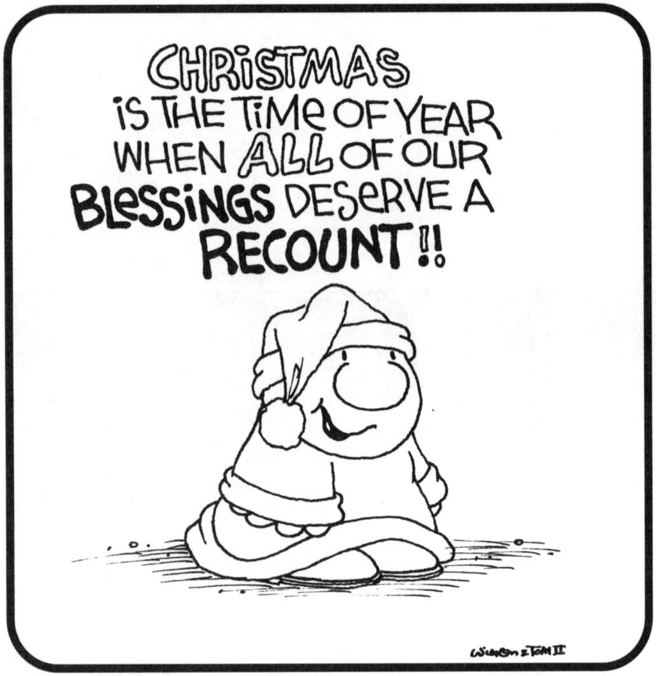
CHRISTMAS IS THE TIME OF YEAR WHEN ALL OF OUR BLESSINGS DESERVE A RECOUNT!!

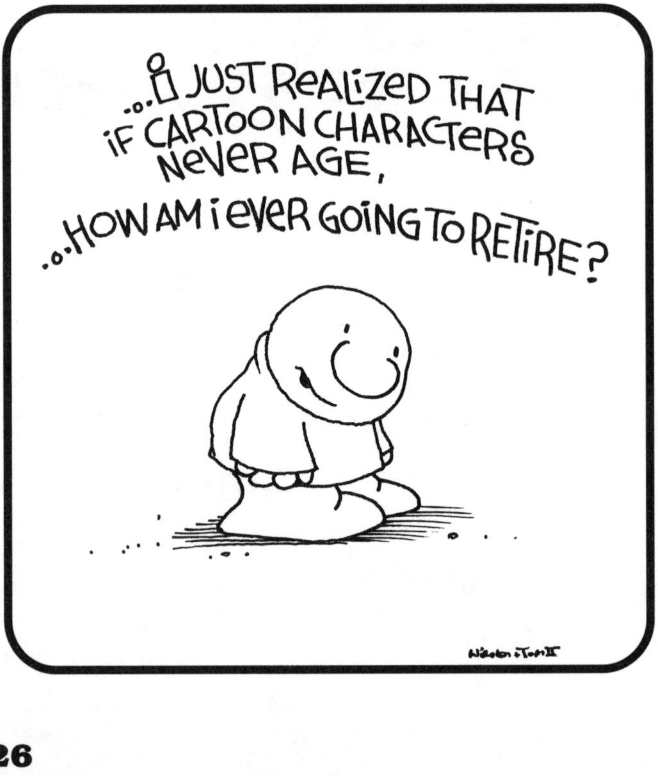
..o..I JUST REALIZED THAT IF CARTOON CHARACTERS NEVER AGE,
..o..HOW AM I EVER GOING TO RETIRE?

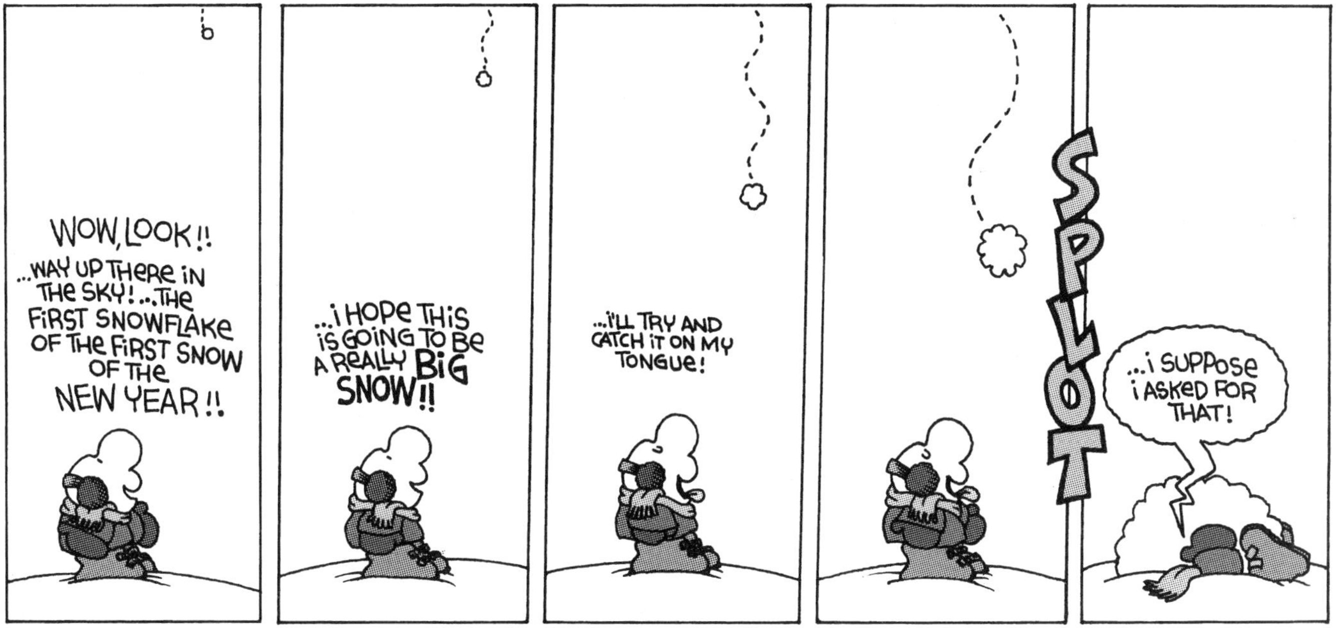
WOW, LOOK !!
...WAY UP THERE IN THE SKY! ..THE FIRST SNOWFLAKE OF THE FIRST SNOW OF THE NEW YEAR !!
...I HOPE THIS IS GOING TO BE A REALLY BIG SNOW!!
...I'LL TRY AND CATCH IT ON MY TONGUE!
SPLOT
...I SUPPOSE I ASKED FOR THAT!

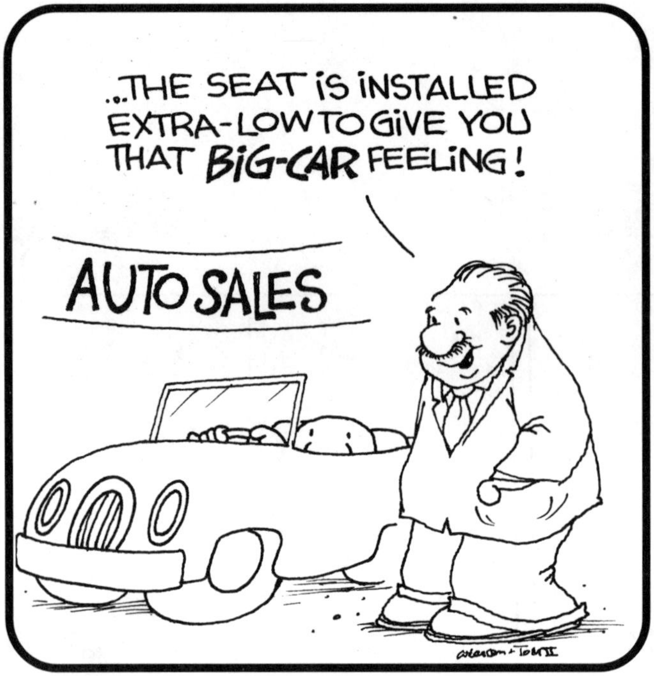
..THE SEAT IS INSTALLED EXTRA-LOW TO GIVE YOU THAT BIG-CAR FEELING!
AUTO SALES

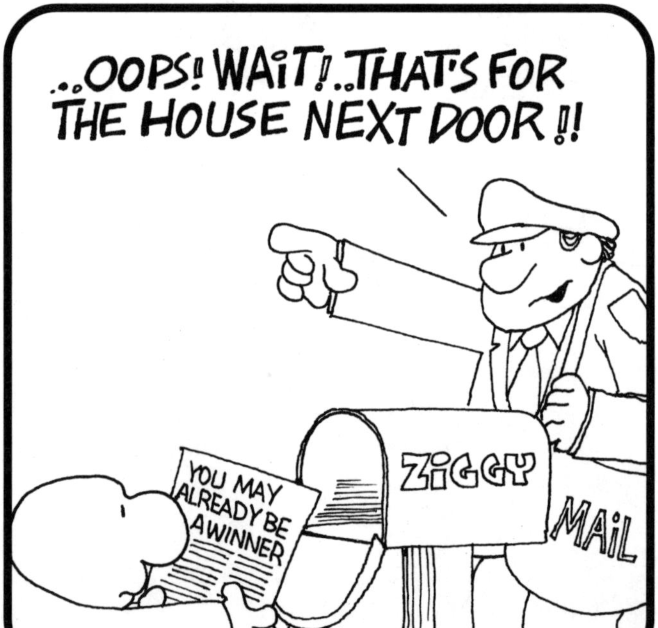
..OOPS! WAIT!..THAT'S FOR THE HOUSE NEXT DOOR!!
YOU MAY ALREADY BE A WINNER
ZIGGY
MAIL